Landscaping with Native Plants of the Intermountain Region

Contributors:

Compiled by:
Hilary Parkinson
Boise State University Horticulture Program
Boise, ID

Edited by:
Ann DeBolt
US Forest Service
Rocky Mountain Research Station
Boise, Idaho

Roger Rosentreter, PhD
USDI Bureau of Land Management
Idaho State Office
Boise, Idaho

Valerie Geertson
USDI Bureau of Land Management
Lower Snake River District
Boise, Idaho

Additional Assistance from:

Michelle Richman, Boise State University Horticulture graduate and BLM intern who developed
the initial Quick Reference Guide on which this publication is based.

Leslie Blackburn
Horticulture Program Head, Boise State University

Printed By

United States Department of the Interior
Bureau of Land Management
Idaho State Office
1387 S. Vinnell Way
Boise, ID 83709

Technical Reference #1730-3

Table of Contents

Native Plant Guide

Additional Information

Introduction

Whether for beauty, drought tolerance, wildlife, or hardiness, homeowners in the arid west are beginning to look to natives as alternatives for their landscaping needs. Each year, more visitors to the native plant gardens at the BLM in Boise, Idaho are asking questions about the plants featured: their names, how to grow, and where to find them. In response to the enthusiasm over native plants and to encourage their use, this guide is meant to aid in their selection, placement, and growth. This guide was conceived and compiled by southwest Idaho gardeners with experience growing native plants. For the purposes of this guide, we have defined a "native plant" as one that evolved in a particular area, and is therefore naturally adapted to its climate and soil. Many of the recommended plants are native to the Boise area, but all of the plants presented here are native to the Intermountain Region, the Southwest, or the Great Plains. The plants featured were selected for their relative ease of growth (assuming they are grown according to recommended cultural conditions), availability, and ornamental value. Because native plants should never be removed from the wild, a list of reputable sources is provided from which most can be obtained.

The format of this guide is subdivided into wildflowers, grasses, shrubs, and trees. Above the scientific and common name, symbols are used for quick reference to provide the following information: sun exposure, water requirements, pollinators it will attract (hummingbirds, butterflies, etc.), whether deciduous or evergreen, and its lowest USDA cold hardiness zone. Additional information is presented in roughly the following order in the text: height and width, color and time of bloom, unusual characteristics or cultural preferences (such as preferred soil conditions), value to wildlife when applicable, and any significant cultural, medicinal, or homeopathic uses, past or present. To quickly search for plants with specific criteria such as height, bloom time, or color, go to the Quick Reference Guide which follows the section on trees.

Many are discouraged from using native plants because they've heard they are too finicky. Without modifying water use, or planting them according to their cultural require-ments, many of these plants can indeed become finicky. To be successful, you'll need to become well acquainted with your landscape: areas of high exposure, areas of shade, drainage, soil type, and microclimates. Once you've mapped it out in your mind, or ideally on paper, you can begin to match the specifics of the site with the cultural needs of the plants. When grown in the appropriate conditions, native plants should be very hardy, rarely needing fertilizers or insecticides.

The first year or two will require a little patience. The first spring and summer will not offer a dense show of foliage and color. Some plants require several years before blooming, and some are slow growing, which may be a drawback for those wanting immediate effect, but it can also be a real bonus when considering the reduced amount of pruning and trimming required. The first and possibly second year will require nearly the same water and weeding as a traditional garden. Because the soil has been turned up at planting time, and watering will be frequent to get the plants established, weeds may be particularly pesky. As the native plants become established, time spent watering will decrease which will dramatically decrease weed growth. Within a few years, the benefits will become apparent in their various forms: healthy beautiful plants, an increase in native birds and other pollinators, a lower water bill, and reduced use of chemicals in the environment.

We hope this manual inspires both novice and experienced gardeners to start or expand the use of natives. Whether integrating drought tolerant plants into a cheatgrass hillside behind the house or creating a special bed to feature native plants, please share your experiences, recommendations, or any other feedback by writing to the Idaho Native Plant Society at: **www.IdahoNativePlants.org**.

Key to Symbols

Sun	Water	Wildlife	Deciduous or Evergreen
= Full Sun	= Drought tolerant	= Attracts butterflies	**D** = Deciduous
= Partial Sun	= Low water	= Attracts bees and insects	**E** = Evergreen
= Shade	= Moderate water	= Attracts birds	**SE** = Semi-Evergreen
	= Plentiful water	= Attracts hummingbirds	**WI** = Winter Interest

USDA Zones

USDA	Fahrenheit (degrees)	USDA	Fahrenheit (Degrees)
1	Below -50	6b	-5 to 0
2a	-50 to -45	7a	0 to 5
2b	-45 to -40	7b	5 to 10
3a	-40 to -35	8a	10 to 15
3b	-35 to -30	8b	15 to 20
4a	-30 to -25	9a	20 to 25
4b	-25 to -20	9b	25 to 30
5a	-20 to -15	10a	30 to 35
5b	-15 to -10	10b	35 to 40
6a	-10 to -5	11	above 40

From Mountain States Wholesale Nursery

Disclaimer: any info on homeopathic or medicinal uses is not meant to instruct or encourage use or consumption of the plants in this manner. Always consult an expert before using any plant for medicinal or homeopathic use.

Wildflowers

 E 3

Achillea millefolium **Western Yarrow**

White flowers fading to cream bloom in dense, round topped clusters from spring to fall on this common wildflower. Some consider it weedy because in moist conditions it self-seeds and spreads rhizomatously (1-3$^1/_2$' tall by 8-12" wide). To keep it more restrained and compact cut back in half after the first bloom, reduce irrigation and divide in the spring. Its prolific habits may be seen as an advantage if used as an alternative to grass. By allowing the dense fern-like foliage to fill in those areas with light foot traffic, it can be mowed and watered less often than a typical lawn. It can be grown in almost any soil. Native Americans used it to make a tea, as an ointment for cuts, burns and bruises, smoked the flowers to clear the head, and placed a wad of the leaves in the ear for ear aches (Ogle 1997). Widespread from lowlands to alpine and subalpine habitats.

E 6

Agave parryi **Parry's Agave**

The light gray to green foliage is broad and flat, growing from a basal rosette (radiating outwards from a central base). It looks similar in form to "Hens and Chicks" but in a much larger version. It typically stands 24" tall by 30" wide, and is lightly toothed at the margins with dark spines at the tip. It adds contrast both in shape and outline, making an excellent specimen for a hot, dry site. Adequate drainage is essential, especially in colder climates. It will take 8 years or more to flower, and will create numerous offshoots throughout the growth period. Native Americans of the southwest ate the younger leaves and heart, used the stalk and fiber to make fire, and cooked the juice to make mescal (wine). It ranges from AZ to NM, and south into Mexico, occurring in open grasslands, pine-oak woodlands, and Arizona chaparral at elevations of 3,600' to 8,400'.

Anaphalis margaritacea

 D 4

Anaphalis margaritacea **Pearly Everlasting**

Ranging in height from 6-18", these cheerful white flowers bloom prolifically from June to September followed by fluffy seed heads, and may be left in the garden for winter interest. Being rhizomatous it can be used as a non-aggressive ground cover and will grow in poor soils. It makes an excellent dried flower, and looks nice in both formal and informal settings. Widespread in forested habitats.

 D 2

Antennaria spp. **Rosy Pussytoes**

Upright flower stalks reach 4-8" with pink and white flowers during June and July. The silver, mat-like foliage is low growing and can be used as a ground cover for areas with light foot traffic, between paving stones, and at the front of a border. It prefers well-drained soil, but can adapt to many different soil types. This plant is drought tolerant (the plant may go dormant, causing the leaves to die back under extreme drought). There are a number of species available with similar growth habit and needs, including *A. microphylla, A. parvifolia, A. dimorpha* and others. Native range spans east of the Cascades in WA, ID, MT, NV, and northern CA in sagebrush to shallow rocky soils.

Aquilegia caerulea

Aquilegia caerulea **Colorado Blue Columbine**

This plant is unique for its long nectar spurs on blue and white blooms that appear from June to August. The size ranges from 12-30" tall by 9-18" wide. It does well in a moist place with partial sun, particularly in the late afternoon. Soil should be moderately fine for adequate drainage.

Aquilegia formosa **Western Columbine**

Growing slightly taller than Aquilegia caerulea, this species can reach 2-3' by 18" wide. It has the same unique flower, but in red and yellow. It blooms from spring to summer. Western Columbine prefers medium to coarse soil and a cooler location with moderate water.

Aster spp. **Wild Aster**

Aster spp.

Purple, light blue to cream flowers bloom at various times of the year, depending on the species, on relatively compact upright plants. Height varies, but is typically between 12"-36" depending upon cultural conditions. Numerous species and cultivars are available. *A. alpinus* grows 6-12" and blooms in the spring, *A. divaricatus* grows 2-3', taking sun or shade, and *A. oblongifolius* grows 16" and thrives in harsh, dry conditions in full sun, blooming in the fall.

Balsamorhiza sagittata **Arrowleaf Balsamroot**

Tender leaf shoots of silvery velvet emerge in April or May, prior to the unfurling of large deep green, basal, arrowhead shaped leaves. Plants eventually grow 18" wide, with numerous 12-24" tall flower stalks. Each stalk carries a single flower head of golden petals surrounding a darker center. Plants don't flower until they are about five years old. It provides spring forage for deer and elk, and grows well on hot dry slopes once established. A few weeks after flowering the foliage will begin to dry up and die as the plant goes dormant until the following spring. It is a good idea to mark the location, so the large taproot is not accidentally dug up in the summer or fall when the plant is without foliage. It is native from lowland to mid elevations in the mountains, and is widespread east of the Cascades.

Balsamorhiza sagittata

Camassia quamash **Blue Camas**

Camassia quamash

The flower consists of six distinct, narrow blue petals pointing straight outwards to form a star pattern, in the center of which is six bright yellow stamens. The plants grow 1-2' x 1-2', bloom from mid-May to June, and prefer fine to coarse soil where very moist springs are followed by relatively dry summers. To the Native Americans of the Northwest, the root was indispensable as a food source.

Lewis and Clark's fortunate encounter with the Nez Perce Indians in September of 1805 meant their very survival. The Nez Perce Indians knew the appropriate time to dig the camas root and numerous ways to prepare it (Phillips 2003). Conflicts over the harvesting of this plant precipitated the Sheepeater Indian War in Idaho. A local endemic species, Cusick's Camas, *Camassia cusickii*, is much larger and prefers heavy clay soils over basalt bedrock. It grows along the Snake River north of Weiser to the Halfway, OR area and in the Blue Mountains. It has been used by the horticulture industry and can be obtained commercially from farm raised plants. It has twice the chromosome number of the common camas and produces more leaves. As noted for Blue Camas, Cusick's Camas also prefers moist conditions in the spring, followed by a dry summer. Blue Camas ranges from British Columbia south to California and east to southwest Alberta, MT, WY and UT.

Echinacea purpurea Purple Coneflower

Blooming from summer to autumn, this sturdy wildflower grows 2-3' tall by 1-2' wide. It is unparalleled for its continuously blooming, stunning purple ray flowers and the raised golden brown center of disk flowers. The root and rhizomes are harvested for their medicinal use to bolster the immune system. Adaptable to many soil conditions, a long slender taproot provides a moderate drought tolerance once established. Native to the Great Plains where it and its relative, *E. angustifolia*, are subjected to over-harvesting.

Erigeron compositus

Erigeron compositus Cut-leaf Daisy

This small wildflower (6" tall) produces numerous white to lavender flowers with yellow centers on short, single stalks in spring. The leaves are divided at the tips, almost fern like, and covered in hairs. The short stature and wooly texture protect this plant from the blazing sun and constant wind of its native habitat of sagebrush deserts to subalpine mountain ridges. This makes it excellent for rock gardens or exposed slopes with good drainage. The genus name *Eri* is Greek for early; and *geron*, old man, like an old man's gray whiskers (Phillips 1997). The common name comes from its use as an insect repellant, where it would be hung in the house or burned to repel fleas and other insect pests (Ogle 1997). There are three varieties: some are found along sandy riverbanks at low elevations in WY, OR and adjacent ID, while others grow at moderate to high elevations in the Rocky Mountains.

Eriogonum heracleoides Wyeth Buckwheat

The low-growing (6-16" tall and wide) perennial forb blooms in late spring to early summer. It has creamy white flowers produced on an erect stalk, green ovate basal leaves with a wooly or pubescent underside, and a whorl of leaves below the flowers. Wyeth buckwheat is very drought tolerant and semi-evergreen. It is one of the many *Eriogonums* that could be used more frequently in landscaping. The flower stalks are brittle once dry and do not tolerate foot traffic. Found in ID, MT and UT.

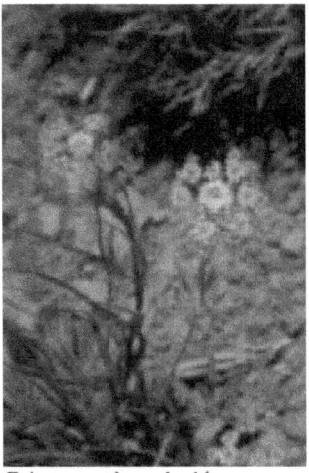

Eriogonum heracleoides

Eriogonum niveum Snow Buckwheat

The flower stalk typically branches 3 ways at the base and splits twice again farther up. Plants range from 6-18" tall and wide. In the summer and fall, white flowers appear in clusters where the branches fork. The foliage is wooly gray and typically 6" tall. Grow for a nice ground cover on slopes and hillsides and for erosion control. It provides a good source of late season nectar for honeybees and food for mule deer and elk. The cultivar "Umatilla" has improved vigor and growth (Ogle 1997). It requires well drained soils and is native from sagebrush deserts to ponderosa pine forests, mostly east of the Cascade Mts, from southern BC to south central OR and into west central ID.

Eriogonum umbellatum with dark yellow flowers (left),
E. heracleoides with creamy flowers (right)

 **SE 3**

Eriogonum umbellatum Sulfur Buckwheat

Yellow flowers with hints of reddish orange or cream bloom profusely above the erect, spatula-shaped leaves in June and July. The semi-evergreen foliage reaches 6"x 6", is deep green and woollier on the underside. The flowers are 12" tall on leafless stalks, although leafy bracts surround the base of each flower. Within 3-5 years, it can spread 2-3' wide. Plant in moderately coarse, well-drained soil. Commercial availability has grown recently as xeriscapers and native plant enthusiasts recognize its many attributes: semi-evergreen foliage, nice in dried flower arrangements, good fall structure and moderate drought tolerance. Native to sagebrush deserts, and alpine rocky ridges, mostly east of the Cascades, from southern British Columbia to CA, east to MT, WY, CO and AZ.

Eriophyllum lanatum

 **D 3**

Eriophyllum lanatum Woolly Sunflower

The 6-12" tall perennial has yellow flowers that bloom in spring. The leaves have a gray green color from the densely matted, soft wooly hairs. Requires a well drained to coarse textured soil and full sun. Plants are drought tolerant and commercially available from several nurseries. It occurs from lowland to mid elevations from BC to CA and east to MT, ID and UT.

 **D 3**

Gaillardia aristata Blanket Flower

This perennial wildflower grows to 24"x 24" with flower rays a mix of red, yellow or orange, blooming from summer to fall. Drought tolerant in moderate to well drained soils once established. Looks excellent when clustered in groups, While short lived, it reseeds easily and is deer resistant. Native intermittently east of the Cascades at 5,000'- 9,000' in open meadows, hills and plains.

 **D 2**

Geranium viscosissimum Sticky Geranium

Growing 12-30" tall and wide, the showy flowers dot grassy mountain slopes from May to September. The petals are pink to lavender, with dark red veins. Opposite leaves are deeply lobed and serrated, and covered with sticky hair. The genus is also known as Crane's Bill for the elongated seedpod. Medicinally they are used to tone up the muscles of the digestive tract, reduce diarrhea and heal sores in the mouth (Ogle 1997). Native east of the Cascades on fairly dry to moist sites with two varieties: var. *viscosissimum* ranging from BC to northern CA, northern NV, and east to Saskatchewan and northern WY, while var. *nervosum* stretches farther southeast into CO and UT.

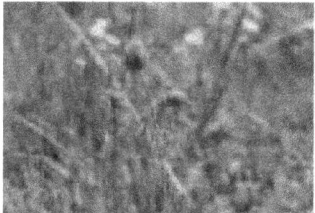 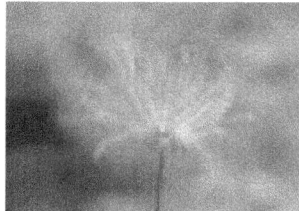

Geum triflorum in bud (left), seed head (right)

 **D 2**

Geum triflorum Prairie Smoke

Also known as old man's whiskers, this reddish to purplish flowered perennial does best in full sun to partial shade in well-drained soils. While moderately drought tolerant, it will do much better with regular irrigation. Without flowers the height is relatively short (6-8"), but in bloom, the stalks can reach up to 18". Native to upland meadow habitats from sagebrush plains to subalpine ridges, it occurs east of the Cascades from British Columbia to California, east to New-foundland, NY, IL, and south to the Rocky Mountain States.

Hesperaloe parviflora (foliage, left), summer flowers (right)

 **E 5**

Hesperaloe parviflora Texas Red Yucca

Reaching 4' tall by 3' wide, this slow growing yucca-like plant produces red blooms in summer that can reach 5' tall. Its leaves are long and narrow and have a gray green color, but are not sharp like yucca. The tubular flowers prove to be hummingbird favorites, and the large black seeds that follow are easy to germinate. Requiring coarse soil, it will rot in heavy clay soils without adequate drainage. Very drought tolerant and widely used in the southwest US, it is a native of TX.

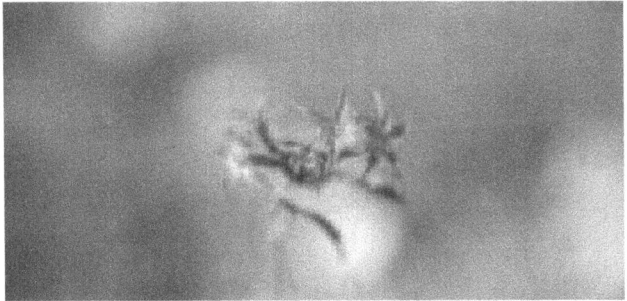

Ipomopsis aggregata

 D 2

Ipomopsis aggregata **Scarlet Gilia**

Red or scarlet flowers bloom in June on this biennial wildflower that grows 12-24" tall. Hummingbirds are attracted to the clusters of long (³/₄"-1¹/₂"), narrow flowers that flare at the tip, forming a six petaled star pattern. It does very well on dry eastern slopes, and while short lived, it should spread by seed and reseed easily. Native to dry meadows, open forests, and rocky slopes from mid-elevations to lower subalpine zones.

Linum perenne var. *lewisii*

 D 3

Linum perenne **Wild Blue Flax**

An 8-24" forb with blue flowers that bloom all spring and summer, though each 5-petaled flower only lasts a single day. Blue flax is easy to grow in full sun, and is often included in wildflower seed mixes. It produces a lot of seed and can be invasive if the site is well watered. It stays green into the summer, is drought tolerant, and can be used to decrease the fire hazard around the home or on steep hillsides. It also looks nice in a border or naturalized setting. Native Americans ate the tasty and nutritious seeds, while the Shoshone used the plant for sore eyes and swelling (Phillips 1999). The variety *lewisii*, native to the western states, is not as invasive as the variety *perenne*, of Eurasian origin.

Lupinus argenteus

 D 5

Lupinus argenteus **Silver Lupine**

From mid-spring to early summer, blue to white sweet pea-like flowers line each flower stalk. The silvery gray foliage with palmate leaves is 8-24" tall x 12-18" wide. In symbiosis with specific bacteria, the roots have a nitrogen-fixing capacity, allowing them to thrive in otherwise poor soil. Due to its long, deep taproot, lupine is very difficult to transplant. Over-grazing increases stands of Silver Lupine. Because of its poisonous alkaloids, sheep and cattle will eat nearly everything but the Lupine, often depleting plant diversity. For landscape use, plant in clumps in beds or mixed borders or naturalized plantings on a hillside. It may be difficult to find commercially. Seeds can be collected while the pod is still green and then air dried to maturity (when collecting never take more than 1/3 of the seeds and correctly identify the plant to verify it is not rare or endangered). Native from pine forests to subalpine ridges of central OR, northeast CA, east to Alberta, the Dakotas, Rocky Mountain States and south to NM.

 D 4

Oenothera missouriensis **Missouri Evening Primrose**

The yellow flowers, each with 4 petals up to 4" across, bloom from June to late September. Plants grow 6-12" tall and often spread 3-4' wide, sometimes very aggressively. Flowers are slightly fragrant, begin blooming in the evening, and last only through the following day. Great as a groundcover on dry sites, and a food source for birds and butterflies. Tolerates poor soil on dry sites once established. Native to NE, TX and MO.

Opuntia spp.

 **E 5**

Opuntia spp. **Prickly Pear Cactus**

Two to three or more pads grow off the base pad at various angles. The pad's shape gives it another common name, Beaver Tail Cactus. It generally reaches no more than 12" tall, but the cluster can spread up to 3' wide. Showy 1½-3½" wide flowers bloom in shades of yellow, pink or red in June/July. White, needle-like, ¼-4" long spines cover the pads. It can form a groundcover in the driest, harshest, most difficult sites. To propagate, remove a pad at the joint, allowing the wound to dry and callous for 2-3 weeks and then shallowly plant in soil. It will root wherever the pad is in contact with soil. It tolerates thin, highly alkaline soils and is native from the plains and foothills to lower mountains in the western states from British Columbia to TX and AZ.

Notes on the following *Penstemon* species

Penstemon is the largest genus of flowering plants endemic to North America, with approximately 270 species. Most penstemons prefer the drier regions of the west, and virtually all require good soil drainage and full sunlight for at least part of the day. Seldom browsed by livestock or wildlife, they attract a variety of pollinators such as bees, hummingbirds and moths. If the flower is long and narrow, it most likely attracts hummingbirds, whereas if wider towards the mouth, something larger than the hummingbird's beak, such as a bee or insect is the more likely candidate (Nold 1999). Most can be grown relatively easily from seed, but often require a prolonged cold moist environment to break dormancy (such as three months in the fridge in a moist media or seeded outside in the fall for natural stratification). Gravel mulch as opposed to bark will encourage self-seeding by holding moisture but preventing rot. Although they may self-seed under the right conditions, there should be no concern of them becoming weedy or invasive. Penstemons have largely been ignored by flower gardeners and commercial nurseries in the US until relatively recently. Commercial availability in local garden centers and catalogs is beginning to rise as admiration over their stunning flowers and low water needs grow. Being a large genus with numerous species, the avid wildflower enthusiast will find it handy to have a book

devoted to penstemons that will explain the terminology and specific flower structures necessary to identify them to species. Check the sources or recommended reading section at the end of the manual for recommendations.

 **D 4**

Penstemon angustifolius **Pagoda Penstemon**

Angustifolius refers to the narrow leaves on this medium sized species that reaches approximately 1' tall x 1' wide. It can have one to many stems per plant. Blooming in summer, the flowers completely encircle the stem, and the colors come in various shades of blue to lavender, paler on the inside with nectar guides. There are four subspecies, one of which comes in pink (var. *dulcis* found in sand dunes of western Utah) (Nold 1999). Often growing in deep sand, it can grow extremely long roots to reach water. Its range spans the Great Plains from eastern MT and the Dakotas to CO east of the Rocky Mountains (Strickler 1997).

 **D 4**

Penstemon barbatus **Scarlet Bugler**

This penstemon can be recognized by its long, linear leaves and distinctly bright red corolla with a strongly reflexed lower lip. Not a long-lived plant, it grows to 2-3' tall by 1-2' wide, but tends to topple if over watered. It flowers from June to September and is a parent to a number of hybrids. One of the most widely available species, it is native to southern UT, CO, to AZ, NM and west TX.

 **D 5**

Penstemon cyaneus **Dark Blue Penstemon**

A dark blue to violet flower, paler on the inside, blooms from late May to early August. The strong, thick stems, woody at the base, grow 12-28" tall and spread to a similar width. The flowers are 1-1.5" long and ½" wide at the mouth. To differentiate it from *P. cyanthus,* a similar species, the anther should be twisted and S-shaped. Native to open plains and lower mountains of southern ID, southwest MT and northwest WY (Strickler 1997).

 **D 5**

Penstemon deustus **Hot Rock Penstemon**

Growing 8-18" tall with a similar width, this *Penstemon* blooms from May to July with small, creamy white flowers. Plants tend to be short-lived under cultivation, but may self-seed under the right conditions, such as in a gravel mulch. The name *deustus* means scorched or burned up, and as the name implies, the species has a preference for exposed, rocky sites, particularly basalt scabland and other volcanic areas. Native east of the Cascades from central WA to southwest MT, northwest WY, northwest UT and southern CA.

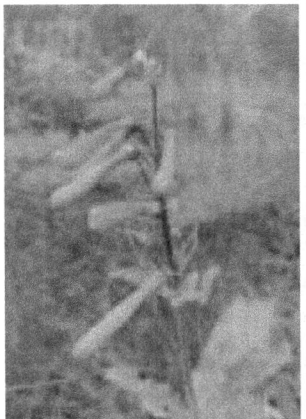

P. eatonii (left), *P. palmeri* (right)

 **D 4**

Penstemon eatonii **Firecracker Penstemon**

A short, woody base produces flower stalks as much as 3' in length (15" wide) lined with bright red flowers that bloom in mid-spring to early summer. The long (1-1 1/2") tubular flowers make superb hummingbird lures. Evergreen basal leaves are a deep shiny green. It is a good species for barren slopes or roadside revegetation projects and grows well from seed. It occurs naturally from southwest CO to NM and southern CA.

 **SE 5**

Penstemon fruticosus **Shrubby Penstemon**

This short evergreen sub-shrub (18" tall x 2' wide) has blue or lavender to light purplish flowers and blooms from May to June. The large, showy flowers are produced on the tips of every branch. It is longer lived than other Penstemons and has three recognized varieties. It requires well-drained soils and occurs throughout the western states east of the Cascades.

 **SE 4**

Penstemon palmeri **Palmer Penstemon**

This showy species is a medium to tall (2-4'x 2'wide) evergreen forb with large, pink, fragrant flowers attractive to bumblebees and hummingbirds. Flowers bloom in late spring and early summer, and the foliage is a blue green color. It is cold hardy and very drought tolerant. While it is short lived, it easily reseeds. Palmer penstemon requires well-drained soil, is a good species for barren slopes, and has been widely seeded on roadsides throughout the western states. Native to southern UT, southern NV, CA and northern AZ (photo on previous page).

 **E 3**

Penstemon pinifolius **Pine-Leaf Penstemon**

This low growing (6-18" by 12-24") evergreen forb has bright red flowers that attract hummingbirds. Adaptable to various soil types, Pine-Leaf Penstemon will flower all summer if irrigated weekly. It is cold hardy, drought tolerant and long-lived. Cultivars with yellow flowers are available as are cultivars with a short, compact growth form. This is an excellent plant for dryland gardens and the pine-like evergreen leaves are bright green even in the middle of winter. Plants can be pruned back in the late spring. Native to NM, southern AZ and northern Mexico.

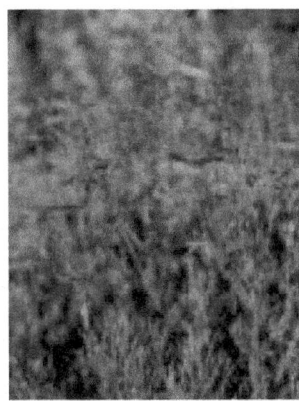

Penstemon pinifolius close-up (left), en masse at 3+ yrs (right)

Penstemon rydbergii

 **D 2**

Penstemon rydbergii **Rydberg's Penstemon**

From May to July flowers bloom on this 8-28" tall plant. It has a similar width. The bluish-purple flowers are gradually inflated towards the mouth and two lipped where the color changes to a velvety white. The plant forms a large basal rosette while the stem leaves are few. Flowers are held horizontally in clusters around the stem, with equal distance between them. There are three recognized varieties. Often found in meadows to moist open slopes, from foothills to mid-elevations in the mountains. Rydberg's Penstemon ranges from central WA to southwest MT, south along the eastern Cascades and Sierras to UT and NM (Strickler 1997).

Penstemon speciosus

Penstemon speciosus Showy Penstemon

Showy Penstemon flowers from May to July. Its large, bright purple to violet flowers fade to a pale blue on the inside, where the lips roll or curl back distinctly. There are typically a few stems per clump, and the leaves are long and linear, the basal ones reaching 2-6". It can survive on less than 12" of precipitation per year, but good drainage is a must. Native to sagebrush steppe and ponderosa pine forests to sub-alpine regions from central and eastern WA to southwest ID, southwest OR, southern CA and northeastern UT (Strickler 1997).

Penstemon strictus Rocky Mountain Penstemon

Plants bloom in June and July and can be moderately long-lived in the garden (to 7 years). This blue to violet penstemon grows 1-3' tall and wide (it spreads via stolons to form clumps). It is a common ingredient of some wildflower mixtures. Its occurrence outside its native range, along highways and other seeded areas has condemned it as an "invasive plant" by some native plant enthusiasts. The cultivar "Bandera" is said to be more tolerant of heavy clay soils. Native to pinyon-juniper, scrub oak, ponderosa pine and aspen communities in south-central and south west WY, eastern UT, western CO, northeast AZ and northwest NM (Nold 1999).

Penstemon venustus Lovely Penstemon

The name "*venustus*" means "beautiful" or "graceful." This stunning 36" tall (with flower stalks) species has medium sized (1¹/2") flowers that range from lavender to purple and bloom from May to June. A key to identification is the spider web-like hair at the end of the filament, unique to this species. The flowers are on one side of the stem, and the leaves, which are lightly serrated, are on the stem only (no basal rosette). The native habitat includes open rock outcrops and gravelly slopes from valleys to the subalpine. Its natural range includes the Blue Mountains of southeast WA and northeast OR and adjacent west-central ID (Strickler 1997).

Penstemon whippleanus Whipple's Penstemon

This species grows 8-24" tall. It blooms in July and August. In the northern part of its range, it is most often found in a creamy white, almost green color; in other areas it may be blue purple to burgundy red. The flowers are unique in that the lower lip is much longer than the upper one. They bloom on one side of the stem (secund), densely crowded in clusters, with 2-7 clusters per stem. There may be only one to a few upright stems per plant. Native to rocky slopes and meadows into alpine regions of southwestern MT, southeastern ID, WY, AZ and UT (Strickler 1997).

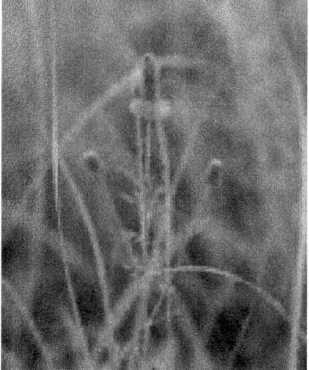

Petalostemon purpureum

Petalostemon purpureum Prairie Clover
(*Dalea purpurea*)

Prairie clover grows 1-2.5' tall, blooming from late May through September. Several stems per plant produce clusters of pinkish purple flowers on elongated spikes. Used in revegetation projects and wildflower gardens for its long bloom season and ability to fix nitrogen. It can easily become overgrazed because it is highly palatable and nutritious to animals. The taproot can be made into a tea to reduce fever in measles patients (http://plants.usda.gov/plants). Native to prairies, along roadsides, and rocky or open woods from IN to Saskatchewan and MT, south to TN and AR.

Solidago spp. **Goldenrod**

This large wildflower reaches 2-5' tall with a similar width, depending on the species. Yellow flowers cover the plant in late summer and early fall. Spreading by underground stems or rhizomes, it can be used as a small deciduous hedge. Prefers full sun and rich soil. *Solidus* is Latin for "to make whole" in reference to its numerous healing properties.

Notes on the following *Sphaeralcea* species

All *Sphaeralcea*, or globemallows, have minute hairs on the leaves that are stellate or star-shaped when viewed with a hand lens. These common plants are not deer resistant, and are difficult to find in areas grazed by livestock because of their palatability. Globemallow is very drought tolerant and readily grown from seed. With the clumps of silver green foliage and abundance of red orange flowers, they seem to rejoice in the heat of the summer, despite poor soil and low water. Within a few years, some species become a dense, multi-stemmed plant that benefits from a grow ring or stakes to keep upright. At a native plant garden in Boise, they are hand watered 4 times per month in the first year, and then only once per month in subsequent years. Over watering will kill them or encourage tall lanky plants that continually flop over. Cutting back after flowering keeps plants more compact and encourages continual blooming. At this time, there is limited commercial availability, usually via seed.

Sphaeralcea ambigua **Desert Globemallow**

More drought tolerant than the other two species listed here and the earliest to bloom, Desert Globemallow typically grows 20-40" tall and wide with orange to brick red flowers in March through June. The gray green foliage typically has 3-5 lobes. Very easy to grow from seed. Native to AZ and NM.

Sphaeralcea spp.

Sphaeralcea grossulariifolia
Gooseberry-leaf Globemallow

A perennial forb with salmon colored flowers that bloom in the summer. Plants range in size from 12-24" tall and wide, depending on the presence of flower stalks. The generic name refers to the Greek word *sphaera*, or sphere, and *alcea* in reference to the round or globose fruits. In this species the leaves are divided nearly to the midvein. Native to ID, OR, NV and UT.

Sphaeralcea munroana **Orange Globemallow**

This 12-24" tall and wide forb with apricot-pink to reddish-orange flowers blooms in the summer. This species has leaves divided or lobed less than halfway to the midvein and is more common at lower elevations than *S. grossulariifolia*. In great contrast to the other two listed here, it does well in clay. It is very drought tolerant and grows readily from seed. Native to ID, NV, UT and CO.

Stanleya pinnata

Stanleya pinnata **Prince's Plume**

Tall in stature, this showy species reaches 3-4' by 18", with spikes of lacy yellow flowers (lacey look from the stamens which extend well beyond the petals) from mid-spring to mid-summer. Numerous stalks branch near the base where the leaves are deeply dissected. Towards the apex, the leaves are more narrow lanceolate to elliptic. As is typical with many Brassicaceae species, the seedpods are long (up to 3") and very narrow. In its natural habitat it is indicative of selenium in the soil. *Stanleya* refers to Lord Edward Stanley (1755-1851) of the Linnaean and Zoological societies in London. Widespread from plains to lower mountains in southeast OR to southern CA, east to the Dakotas, KS and TX.

 **E 3**

Yucca glauca **Narrowleaf Yucca**

Narrowleaf Yucca leaves are long, narrow, and strap-like with spiny tips. The plant grows 2-3' tall and wide, bunched at the base, and then spreads outwards, appearing like a V in profile. Creamy white, pendulous, bell-shaped flowers bloom in July, rising on spikes 3-6' tall. It prefers coarse, well-drained soil, and does well on slopes, surviving harsh, exposed sites with poor soil (the roots can be up to 20' long). The fruit is large and

Yucca glauca

fleshy, the seed glossy and $1/2$" across. Yucca requires a specific insect, the yucca moth, for pollination. The roots and leaves can be used to make soap, the flower stalk eaten like asparagus, and the leaves woven into baskets. Native to deserts and sandy slopes in the southwestern US, north into MT and N. Dakota, east to IA, and southwest to TX and NM.

Grasses

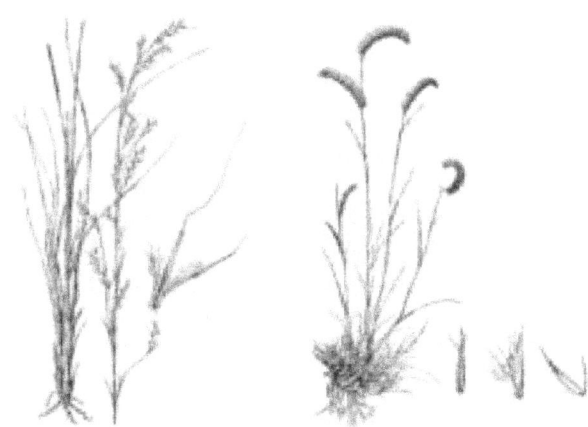

Andropogon scoparium (left), *Bouteloua gracilis* (right)

 **WI 4**

Notes on warm season vs. cool season grasses
Grasses are categorized as warm vs. cool season based on their season of greatest growth. Cool season grasses actively grow in the spring and fall, becoming dormant during the hottest months of summer. Warm season grasses are at their peak during summer, and break winter dormancy later than cool season grasses.

Andropogon scoparium **Little Bluestem**
(*Schizachyrium scoparium*)
This blue green, warm season, tall tufted grass grows approximately 12-36" tall by 18" wide and needs well-drained soil. The decorative seed head forms in summer and matures to a rich, red brown color in the fall. The fall color lasts throughout the winter. It can grow as a bunchgrass in drier areas, or as a ground cover in moister spots. Being non-invasive it will not crowd out surrounding grasses or wildflowers. In restoration projects, it can be used for roadside revegetation projects. While not native to Idaho, it grows well with occasional summer watering. Native habitats are foothills, tall grass prairies, and plains ranging from the east side of the Rocky Mountains to the Great Plains.

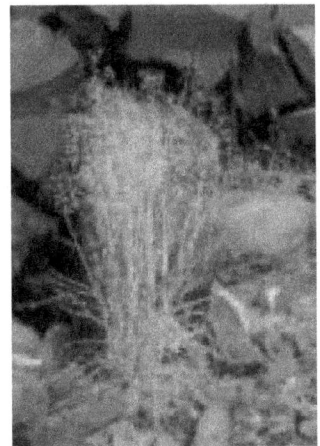
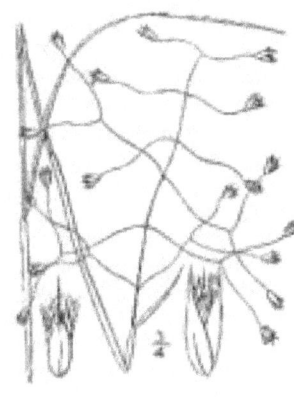

Achnatherum hymenoides

 **WI 5**

 **D 3**

Achnatherum hymenoides **Indian Ricegrass**
(*Oryzopsis hymenoides*)
This warm season, short-lived perennial bunchgrass grows 12-16". It forms a beautiful airy inflorescence when it goes to seed (the small kernel-like seeds are purportedly edible). Besides its ornamental value, this is a great grass for sandy sites. It does not tolerate shade. Cultivars are being developed that retain the seed in the inflorescence, which facilitates collecting. Seeds must be planted 2-3" deep. Native to grasslands, desert plains and foothills, often rocky or sandy soil, ranging from east of the Cascades, British Columbia to southern CA and northeast Mexico, east to the Dakotas and TX.

Bouteloua gracilis **Blue Grama**
Growing only 4-12" tall and wide, this mat-forming, warm season grass can be naturalized to form a fairly dense, grass-like meadow with minimal irrigation once established. For a low water alternative to a thirsty lawn, high success rates have been reported by seeding a mixture of Blue Grama with Buffalo Grass (*Buchloe dactyloides*). It can be mown to a height of 4-6" to encourage sod formation. Requires full sun and well-drained soil. It is a major range grass for animals of the prairies and Great Plains, often associated with buffalograss, wheatgrass and needlegrasses.

 **D 5**

Buchloe dactyloides Buffalograss

This warm season grass has 10-18" long blue-gray to green blades. The actual height is only 3-5" as the blades do not stand erect, but bend and lean over at the nodes. It spreads by vegetative stolons to form a mat 2' wide, which turns reddish in the fall. As discussed above, it can be used in combination with Blue Grama as an alternative to the thirsty Kentucky Blue Grass for low maintenance and low traffic areas. The plant is dioecious, (male or staminate plant is separate from female or pistillate plant). If un-mowed, the male plants have spikes on one side that rise above the leaves, while the female plants have small bundles in the leaf axis, and a blade that is curly and lightly hairy on both sides. It makes a soft, dense lawn if used alone. The widespread roots are often 3-4 feet deep, need-ing only 12" of rain/year once established (or 1/2" every 2 weeks to stay green during summer), and less than 1/3 of the fertilizer of a typical lawn. It can be mowed once a month May through September. It tolerates compacted soil, and prefers clay or clay loam to sand. While it will stay green during the summer given its minimal water require-ments, it will begin to turn tan at the first frost, not greening up until warm weather the following spring. Use treated seed in early spring or after the first frost in fall at 2-3 lb per 1,000 square feet, or sow plugs 1' apart. Consult a specialist regarding appropriate soil preparation and seeding methods for the best results. Native to the central Great Plains regions of short grass prairies, it provides cover and a food source for small rodents, birds and grazing animals.

Buchloe dactyloides (left), *Elymus elymoides* (right)

 **E 4**

Elymus elymoides Bottlebrush Squirreltail
(Sitanion hystrix)

This cool season grass grows 13-24" tall. It develops a unique tufted seed head in mid-spring with awns forming a distinct right angle to the stem, much like a bottlebrush. It is a short-lived, early successional species that grows well after wildfires and other disturbances. It can act as a nurse plant on harsh sites barren of most other vegetation. Native to dry hills, plains, open woods from British Columbia south and east to MS, TX, CA, and Mexico. In the often harsh climates of NV it can survive at elevations ranging from 2,000-11,000' with only 7-20" of rain per year.

 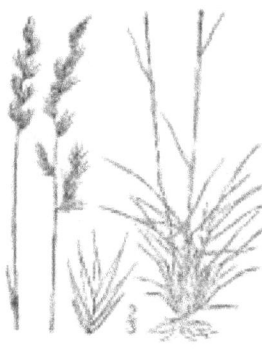

Festuca idahoensis (left), *Festuca ovina* (right)

 **E 4**

Festuca idahoensis Idaho Fescue

Growing 18" tall by 15" wide, this short, tufted bunchgrass with gray-blue blades blooms in early summer. As a cool season grass, it's greatest growth occurs in March and April. It matures in late summer and can have moderate regrowth when provided moisture in the fall. It makes a nice ground cover and weed suppressor and will self-seed easily if the flowering stalks are not mowed or cut back. It is also a terrific specimen plant to use in garden beds. It prefers medium to moderately fine, deep fertile soils and prefers 14" of precipitation per year, but can survive on 11". In the Intermountain Region it is a significant under-story plant in sagebrush and bluebunch wheatgrass zones. Native to grasslands and semi-desert sagebrush communi-ties in the foothills and mountains of the western US.

 **WI 5**

Festuca ovina Sheep Fescue

A cool season, relatively small but long-lived perennial bunchgrass, the flowering stalk grows 18" tall. It is more drought tolerant than *F. idahoensis* and less palatable to livestock and wild game. It is shade and cold tolerant, but does not do well on sites that are continually wet. Use it as a groundcover, in the interspaces of a plant community, for erosion control, and to compete with weeds such as cheatgrass. Widely available in several cultivars including "Covar," which tends to form more seed heads and is a particularly aggressive and drought tolerant selection (Ogle 1997).

Leymus cinereus in June (left), same plant in late winter (right)

 **WI 3**

Leymus cinereus **Great Basin Wildrye**

Great Basin Wild Rye is a cool season, long-lived species that can develop taproots up to 14' deep. Upright bunches reach 4-6' tall and 3' in diameter, and take 2-3 years to become established. The blades are bluish tan with wheat-like seed heads in the summer and fall. Decorative as well as hardy, it is able to withstand fire, drought and flooding. "Magnar" is a bluish green cultivar that demonstrates good seedling vigor, seed production and salt tolerance. Over-grazing during the periods of regrowth in the spring and fall can easily damage Wildrye (Ogle 1997). Common along drainage basins and rocky slopes with a minimum of 10" precipitation in the Intermountain Regions of the western US at elevations up to 8,000 feet.

 **WI 4**

Pseudoroegneria spicata **Bluebunch Wheatgrass**
(*Agropyron spicatum*)

This is a long-lived, cool season bunchgrass that grows 13-24" tall. It is a common, widespread species in most of western North America. As the name implies, the grass has a bluish cast (or blue-green with more water) with a decorative inflorescence. Unfortunately, Bluebunch Wheatgrass has been overgrazed in many areas. It can deter the spread of fire when growing on sites without dense, dried annual grass (unless it is windy or the fire is moving uphill).

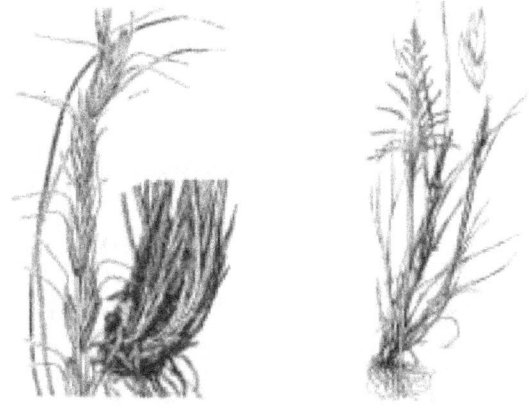

Pseudoroegneria spicata (left), *Sporobolus cryptandrus* (right)

 **WI 4**

Sporobolus cryptandrus **Sand Dropseed**

Sand Dropseed is a warm season, short-lived perennial that grows 8-16" tall. It forms an open, diffuse inflorescence and has a hairy ligule (collar around the top of the grass sheath which surrounds the blade). Sand Dropseed stays green in the heat of the summer and forms a fire resistant area if mowed annually. It has a very small seed and can be aerially seeded on steep slopes. It is common in well drained, sandy to gravelly soils, establishes easily, is drought tolerant and able to withstand moderate grazing. It is an early successional species and does well in disturbed areas. Native to the western states, but not the desert southwest.

Shrubs

☀ ⛅ 💧💧+ 🐝 🐦 **D 3**

Acer glabrum

Rocky Mountain Maple

A shrub to small tree that grows from 8-25' tall by 8' wide. It has 3-5 lobed leaves with double toothed margins. Showy fall foliage varies from red and orange to yellow. This provides a nice substitute for the popular vine maple, which is not as hardy. Rocky Mountain Maple is found from British Columbia to northern CA, and east to ID, MT, UT, WY and northwest CO beneath a coniferous overstory or along streambottoms in forested areas.

⛅ 🔲 💧 🦋 🐝 🐦 **D 4**

Amelanchier alnifolia **Saskatoon Serviceberry**

Amelanchier alnifolia

Showy racemes of pure white flowers adorn this shrub in April to May, followed by purple fruits resembling blueberries. Although size will vary depending upon available water, this shrub ranges from 5-20' tall by 6-15' wide. It is often more broad than tall. The leaf is almost blue green, the shape cordate at base, and the margin slightly toothed toward the apex. The fruits can be used in pies, jams, fruit rolls, for jelly and syrup, or pounded to make mince meat. A special Native American delicacy consisted of salmon eggs and dried serviceberries, not mashed, but served boiled or cold (Turner et al., 1980). In emergencies or times of famine, the juice of the fruits was squeezed over Black Tree-Lichen (*Bryoria fremontii*) to add flavor before drying it. In the landscape, use as a specimen, around a patio or deck, as a shelterbelt, or in a naturalized setting for

a continual show from spring flowers, to summer berries, to spectacular fall color. Native to open woods, canyons and hillsides from southern AK to CA, east to Alberta, the Dakotas, NE, NM and AZ.

 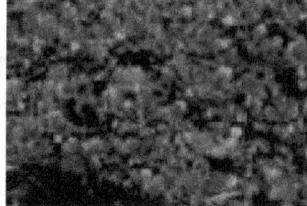

Arctostaphylos uva-ursi (left), close-up (right)

⛅ 🔲 💧 🐝 **E 4**

Arctostaphylos uva-ursi **Kinnikinnick**

Clusters of pink, urn-shaped flowers bloom from March to April on this mat-forming evergreen shrub. The dense mats rarely exceed 6" in height, can spread to 6' wide, and prefer cooler sites with afternoon shade. The 1" long simple, leathery, dark green leaves become slightly reddish-green to purple in the fall. It roots wherever branches touch the soil. While slow growing initially, once established, it is a low maintenance, long lived ground cover. Well-drained soil is essential. Indians used the bark as tobacco and the fruit may attract songbirds and small mammals (Ogle 1997). According to Cronquist (1973) "it is one of the finest ground covers known, especially for dry banks." Ranges from AK to Labrador, south to coastal CA, ID, and MT and throughout the Rocky Mountains.

Artemisia cana

☀ 🔲❗🔲 🐝 🐦 **SE 3**

Artemisia cana **Silver Sagebrush**

This semi-evergreen shrub grows 3-5' tall with a similar width and has inconspicuous yellow flowers that run the length of the stem. It blooms from August to September. The silver foliage has entire, non-lobed leaves and semi-upright branches making it a nice mid-size shrub in a naturalized landscape. It spreads rhizomatously and can root sprout after a fire. It is the second most populous shrub, after Big Sagebrush (*Artemisia tridentata*), in the 11 western states. Native to mountains and higher valleys, it is often in ephemerally moist meadows and drainage ways that become dry by midsummer. Its range spans British Columbia, CA, UT and NM.

Artemisia frigida

 **SE 3**

Artemisia frigida **Fringed Sagebrush**

The finely divided foliage is metallic silver, upright to decumbent, 8-18" tall by 2-3' wide. Small yellow flowers appear in mid to late summer. Within approximately three years, this semi-shrub can withstand short-term drought conditions fairly well. Prior to establishment, it will desiccate easily, preferring a cooler site or shade from surrounding vegetation as it is native to higher elevation sites (> 5,000') in the Intermountain Region. Lightly prune to reduce desiccation and maintain clump growth form. Occurring throughout the western states and Canada, it is the most common sage in Alaska.

 **SE 5**

Artemisia ludoviciana **Louisiana Sage**

While it smells strongly of sagebrush, the light gray branches typically reach only 12-18" tall by 24" wide and the leaves tend to be entire or have irregular margins versus tri-lobed. Small greenish yellow flowers bloom in clusters towards the end of the stems of this sub-shrub from late July to early September. Small desert animals utilize it for cover, and it is a food source for sage grouse, cattle, rabbits, rodents, elk and mountain goats. Besides being a key ceremonial plant for the Cheyenne people, it was formulated in various ways by numerous Native Americans to treat the following ailments: stomach problems, nose bleeds, odors, sinus infections, headaches, long standing sores, menstrual disorders, fever, diarrhea and soar throat. *Artemisia* is poisonous in large doses. It can adapt to numerous conditions, including perennial or ephemeral streams, sagebrush steppe, prairies, and disturbed areas as it spreads rhizomatously. It ranges from east of the Cascades in WA and OR south to Mexico, and throughout the Great Plains States into northeast CA.

 **SE 4**

Artemisia tridentata **Big Sagebrush**

There are three subspecies of Big Sagebrush: ssp. *tridentata*, ssp.*wyomingensis* and ssp. *vaseyana*. Size is highly variable, from 3-12'. All have yellow, inconspicuous flowers that bloom in the fall. While ssp. *tridentata* (Basin Big Sagebrush) is typically the tallest, with pendulous flowers and uneven growth form, ssp. *vaseyana* (Mountain Big Sagebrush) tends to be smaller, with erect flowering branches that form a level, flat top, and a more compact growth pattern. Subspecies *wyomingensis* (Wyoming Big Sagebrush) is the most drought tolerant, grows in shallower soil, produces 3-parted major branches, and grows about three feet tall. All have gray green hairy leaves that are semi-evergreen with approximately one third of the leaves dropping off in late summer. While Big Sagebrush prefers deep, rich, moist alluvial loams, it is very drought tolerant once established and will rot or become tall and leggy if overwatered. The shrub is an excellent selection when creating a wildlife friendly landscape: sage grouse eat the leaves, flowers and fruit; squirrels, rabbits and small rodents eat the leaves and seeds, and antelope, mule deer and mountain sheep eat the leaves and young twigs. The hard dense wood can be used for firewood and purportedly repels mosquitoes when burned. Big Sagebrush covers more acreage in the 11 western states than any other plant. It is native to the plains, desert, hills and lower mountain slopes from British Columbia to Baja, CA, and east to western NE.

Atriplex canescens (in background)

 **E 4**

Atriplex canescens **Four-wing Saltbush**

The grayish-white leaves are long, linear, and covered with microscopic scales giving the leaves a "crystalline" look. The plant typically grows 4-5' tall, but may reach 6' tall by 8' wide. Inconspicuous yellow blooms appear in mid-spring to midsummer. The name comes from the four large bracts, entire to fringed, that appear on the seeds. Seeds can be ground and cooked like cereal, the leaves eaten, and ashes used to leaven bread (Phillips 1998). For wildlife, it is an important browse plant. *Atriplex* spp. have evolved a unique method of accessing water unavailable to other plants. They can take in water with high salt content by storing it in their leaves and then shedding them. They can survive in highly alkaline areas, in sand or clay, shallow or deep soils in desert flats, washes, mesas, ridges, slopes or sand dunes. They range throughout the western US as far east as the Dakotas and south to TX.

Cercocarpus ledifolius (left), leaves (right)

 **E 4**

Cercocarpus ledifolius
Curl-leaf Mountain Mahogany

This evergreen shrub or multi-stemmed tree grows 8-15' tall by 6-8' wide, with dark green, leathery leaves and attractive gray bark. Pale yellow, inconspicuous flowers bloom in May. *Cercocarpus* comes from the Greek *kerkos*, meaning tail, and *carpos*, meaning fruit, in reference to the decorative curly-cue plume that persists throughout the summer and fall as the seeds ripen. The coil helps work the seed into the ground by coiling when damp and straightening when dry (Knopf 1991). The leaves, approximately 1" long and 1/4" wide, have margins that curl inwards (hence the common name, Curl-Leaf). The curled leaf limits the amount of surface area exposed to the sun and wind, helping it survive during hot, dry weather. The dense compact growth form with upright branches provides an excellent drought tolerant evergreen shrub that could be used as a screen year round. Does best in full sun with well-drained soil, and can survive with approximately 10-20" of rain or irrigation per year. The native range spans ID, as far north as southeast WA, south to CA and AZ and east to MT and CO.

D 4

Cercocarpus montanus **Mountain Mahogany**
Also known as Birch-Leaf Mountain Mahogany, white flowers bloom from April to May on this shrub, which grows 5-10' tall by 3-5' wide. It prefers medium to well drained soils, and like *C. ledifolius*, decorative plumes persist into the fall. It provides cover for birds, attracts pollinators, and is a winter browse plant for deer and elk. Tools, such as bows, were made from the wood, and the bark was dried to treat tuberculosis, colds, respiratory

problems, and sores. The Hopi used the bark to make a dye (Mozingo 1997). Native habitats are mountainsides, rocky bluffs, open woodlands, canyons and rim rock from OR to WY, SD, southern CA and central Mexico.

 **SE 4**

Chamaebatiaria millefolium **Fern Bush**
This upright shrub grows 6-8' tall by 4-6' wide bearing elongated clusters of white flowers in summer. While deciduous in cold climates, it re-leafs by late winter. The fern-like foliage resembles yarrow, hence the same species name, *millefolium*. An excellent choice for hot dry

Chamaebatiaria millefolium

exposures, it can even grow in lava fields. It is very drought tolerant once established. Great Basin Indians used it medicinally as a tea for cramps and stomachaches. It may be browsed by sheep and deer, but rarely cattle (Mozingo 1987). Its native range in rocky habitats amidst juniper and pinyon pine includes the eastern side of the Sierra Nevada, north into OR and ID, south to WY, UT and eastern NV.

 **D 3**

Chrysothamnus nauseosus **Rubber Rabbitbrush**
Rubber Rabbitbrush, also known as Gray Rabbitbrush, grows 2-7' tall by 1-4' wide. *Chrys* is Greek for golden yellow, in reference to the dense, dark yellow flowers that cover the bush from late summer into the fall. The long narrow leaves are silvery green and between 1 to 3 inches long. Like Sagebrush, this shrub makes an excellent contrast or accent plant. Rubber Rabbitbrush can resprout after disturbances such as fire. The primary characteristic to distinguish it from the Green Rabbitbrush is the fine wooly hair that can easily be scraped off the stems. The Shoshone of Nevada utilized the shrub for coughs, colds, and to stop diarrhea. The Cheyenne used it dermally for smallpox and to reduce itching (Phillips 1999). The deep roots make it extremely drought tolerant once established. It provides good cover for small rodents and jackrabbits seeking to elude birds of prey and other predators. Native Americans chewed the stems to make a latex gum to relieve hunger and thirst. During rubber shortages of World War II, scientists became interested in the latex and found that a high-quality rubber (called chrysil) could be produced, but not in the high quantities needed at that time (Mozingo 1987). Nevertheless, the name Rubber Rabbitbrush stuck. Native to dry open areas ranging from lowlands to sagebrush steppe to montane forest zones. There are six different varieties that vary morphologically and by range. Collectively, they cover eastern OR, ID, MT, WY and the Great Plains States.

Chrysothamnus viscidiflorus Green Rabbitbrush

A smaller shrub than *Chrysothamnus nauseosus*, it reaches a maximum height of 3', a width of 1-2' and lacks the pubescence or fine wooly hairs on the stems. Leaves are typically green and shiny with glands that give it a sticky texture. Some subspecies have leaves that are twisted lengthwise, and leaves vary from 1/2-2" long. Because both species of rabbitbrush resprout after a fire, germinate easily from seed, and are not the first choice for cattle, they can come to dominate a rangeland damaged by overgrazing or fire (Mozingo 1987). This rabbitbrush is extremely drought tolerant and is found throughout the west.

Cornus stolonifera Red-osier Dogwood

This medium shrub grows 3-9' tall by 5-8' wide, producing white flowers in May or June. Its unusual leaves have veins that curve inwards. It prefers a rich, moist, well-drained soil and may do better with partial shade in hot climates. It makes an excellent shrub for stream stabilization, wind breaks, screens and naturalized landscaping. The berries attract birds and the red branches are very showy in winter. Native throughout the western US, usually along creeks, streams or draws.

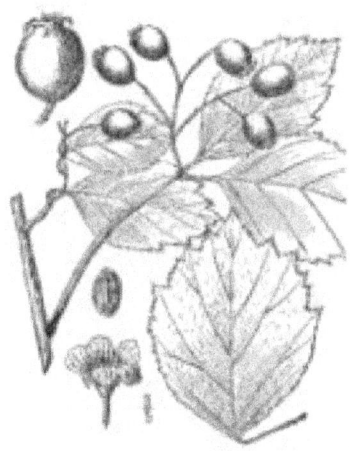

Crataegus douglasii Douglas Hawthorn

This species forms a large shrub or round topped tree 8-20' tall by approximately 15' wide, with showy clusters of globe-shaped white flowers in mid spring. Unlike its cousin, Columbia Hawthorn (*C. columbiana*), the red, shiny thorns are only 1/2" to 1" long, compared to 4" long. Both tolerate a wide range of soil conditions, and can be used to stabilize soil along roads, ditches, and banks. For bird habitat, the thorns create excellent protection from predators and the blue-black berries are a source of food. In their native habitat, they are typically found near streams in sagebrush, bunchgrass and Ponderosa Pine areas, intermixed with Douglas-Fir and Cedar-Hemlock in forest openings. Their range spans the Pacific Northwest, from southern AK to British Columbia and northern CA.

Ephedra viridis

Ephedra viridis Mormon Tea

This unusual looking plant in the joint fir family is a twiggy, upright, leafless, but also evergreen shrub, typically 2-5' tall with a similar width. Dioecious, it forms yellow, flower-like cones and berry-like fruits. It is extremely drought tolerant, requires well drained soil and prefers full sun. It would do well as a background plant, or to provide year round interest with its unique form. The plant produces ephedrine, an allergy and asthma treatment, and a rather controversial stimulant and metabolic enhancer. Early Mormon settlers used it to make tea, unaware of its chemical effects on the body and potential risks for stroke or heart attack. It is a common member of salt desert shrub communities, in highly alkaline, sandy soils in association with Shadscale and Greasewood. It is native to NV, UT and eastern CA.

Fallugia paradoxa

Fallugia paradoxa Apache Plume

A medium tall, semi-evergreen shrub (4-6'tall and wide) that produces white to rose flowers that mature into seeds with feathery plumes. The flowers bloom from late spring through early summer. After the plumes form, they remain on the shrub for several months adding texture and interest. The leaves are wedge shaped and tri-lobed, similar to bitterbrush. It is a nice candidate for an informal hedge or specimen plant. It requires moderately coarse soil that is well-drained and prefers full sun. It is very drought tolerant and does well in the Boise valley, though its natural range is the southwest deserts to the Colorado Plateau.

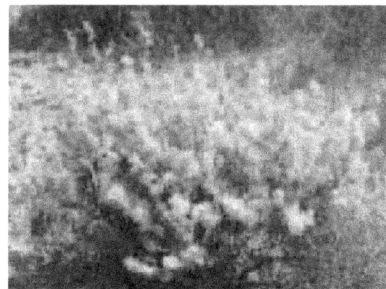
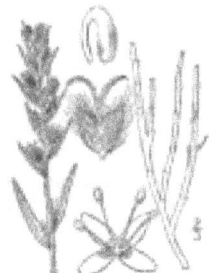

Krascheninnikovia lanata

 **E 3**

Krascheninnikovia (Ceratoides) lanata Winterfat

Densely branched, this compact shrub grows 1-3'with a similar spread. The common name refers to its importance as a browse plant for both livestock and wildlife. The branches, leaves and fruit are covered in dense hair (*lanata*). Leaves are linear and the flowers consist of a dense wooly cluster in spring. Like others in the Chenopodiaceae family, it tolerates highly alkaline soil, but is intolerant of acidic or poorly drained soil. Native to the plains and foothills in WA, OR to CA, east to ID and MT.

 **E 4**

Mahonia repens Creeping Oregon Grape

This low-growing, evergreen sub-shrub or ground cover with holly-like leaves is very drought and shade tolerant. It grows 1' tall by 1-3' wide. The yellow flowers bloom in a raceme in April to May, and the fruit forms a glaucous-blue fruit resembling a blueberry. The compound leaf has 5-7 leaflets, each typically twice as long as broad. Inconspicuous spinulose teeth again mimic the holly, while the leaf surface is glossy to dull on the upper side and dull on the lower side. This is one of the few plants that can grow well in dry shade, in clay to loam soils. The tart fruits can be used to make jelly, wine, or lemonade. Native Americans used the yellow bark to make dyes and medicinally to ease childbirth, heal infections, fight venereal diseases, and treat kidney problems. Modern herbalists use it to reduce fevers, lower inflammations and infections, reduce indigestion, and to treat liver and gall bladder disorders. By isolating the alkaloid berberine from the yellow sap in the twigs, researchers have found an antibiotic mechanism that can fight a broad range of bacteria (Phillips 1999). Widespread in the western US and Canada.

 **D 5**

Philadelphus lewisii Mockorange, Syringa

Idaho's state flower is a lovely deciduous shrub growing 4-10' tall by 6-8' wide with showy, 4 petaled white flowers. They bloom in late spring to early summer. Leaves are ovate to elliptic with entire to serrate margins on oppositely branched stems. The flowers are borne singly on stems or in loose terminal clusters, and are incredibly fragrant (similar to orange blossoms). Syringa grows best in well-drained

soils and is quite drought tolerant, but prefers more water in the spring. Shrubs grow from 2,000' to 7,000' in elevation along waterways, on cliffs, talus slopes and rocky hillsides. Its range spans British Columbia to northern CA, from the coast to Montana and north and central ID.

Philadelphus lewisii

 **D 3**

Physocarpus malvaceus Ninebark

This deciduous shrub grows 3-6' tall and wide. Its white flowers are in terminal corymbs in the spring. The branches are alternate; leaves are palmately 3-5 lobed turning beautiful shades of red in the fall. The bark often has stripes and may peel, hence the name, Ninebark. Native to canyons, hillsides, grasslands in Ponderosa Pine and Douglas Fir forests east of the Cascades from southern British Columbia to ID, OR, WA, MT, WY and UT.

Potentilla fruticosa

 **D 3**

Potentilla fruticosa Shrubby Cinquefoil

This dense shrub grows 3' tall by 3' wide with small, palmately compound, flat, narrow to elliptic leaves. One inch yellow flowers adorn the shrub from early summer to mid fall. Shorter varieties grow at higher elevations, or on extreme windy slopes. Shrubby Cinquefoil is widely used in the landscape industry today. Those with anything but yellow blooms, such as white, fawn, orange, or red are introduced from Eurasia. It grows at higher elevations from the mountain hemlock zone to beyond the timberline. The range spans AK south to CA, east through the Rocky Mountain States to Labrador, Nova Scotia, NJ and PA.

Prunus emarginata flowers (left), fruit (right)

Prunus emarginata **Bitter Cherry**

Typically 6-8' tall by 4-6' wide, this shrub produces fragrant, white flowers in spring and red cherries in late summer and fall. For fruit production, at least two plants must be present. The leaf edge is finely toothed like the Chokecherry, but smaller and more obtuse at the tip. Foliage turns yellow in the fall. The bark is smooth and silvery gray. Because it will send up suckers it may spread beyond its designated area or need to be pruned back. It prefers well-drained soil and a sunny location. It does not do well in the shade of competing vegetation. Establishing easily on disturbed sites, it can be used to control erosion and stabilize soil. The bark smells like cherry when crushed, but has a bitter taste. Native Americans used the bark to make watertight baskets, ropes, arrows, and as a treatment for tuberculosis. A contraceptive was made from rotting wood. A treatment for cancer, hydrogen cyanide, is found in the leaves and seeds (NRCS Plants Database 8/2003). Deer and elk make use of the shrub for food and cover. It ranges from the edge of the Great Basin north into British Columbia, and east to ID and MT, often in large stands on steep rocky slopes or less dense groups along streams or valley bottoms.

Prunus virginiana **Chokecherry**

This shrub to small tree typically grows 10-20' tall by 8-10' wide (spreading vegetatively). It has finely toothed 3" long leaves. White flowers bloom on 6" pendulant spikes in spring. Colorful red fruits ripen to a deep purple in the summer. The seeds are spread by birds. At certain times of the year, the plant may be toxic to livestock due to the hydrocyanic acid in the foliage (Mozingo 1987). While incredibly bitter, the fruit can be collected and made into excellent syrup or jelly. Chokecherry is widespread throughout the US and Canada with two varieties. Variety *melanocarpa* is the larger of the two (12-20') and has a drupe (type of fruit) that is deep bluish-purple to black. It occurs from British Columbia to CA, east to Alberta and the Dakotas and south to the Rocky Mountain States and NM. Variety *demissa* typically grows 6-12', and has a black drupe. It is found west of the Cascades from British Columbia to northwest OR.

Purshia tridentata flowers

Purshia tridentata **Antelope Bitterbrush**

Yellow, highly fragrant flowers cover this shrub in late April and May. It grows 5-8' tall by 4-6' wide, with dense alternate branching, and is very drought tolerant once established (overwatering may kill it). The wedge shaped leaves, with three deep lobes, are similar to Apache Plume, except the upper leaf surface is green, the lower one covered in dense hairs. It attracts birds and insects and is an important food source for big game and livestock, particularly during the winter. Each flower produces one large black seed, often spread by rodents. Native habitat ranges from sagebrush deserts to Ponderosa Pine forests from British Columbia to CA, east of the Cascades to ID, MT, CO and NM.

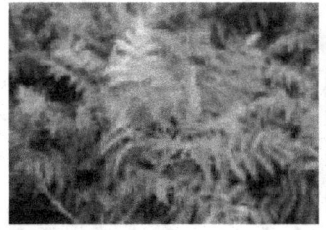

Rhus glabra

Rhus glabra **Smooth Sumac**

Compound, blue green leaves turn red in fall on this 4-20' tall bushy shrub with reddish purple stems. Male flowers are bluish-white, while female flowers are greenish red. They bloom in the summer, and form hairy red fruit in the fall. Spreads by rhizomes and may be considered weedy, but also popular as an ornamental. Native east of the Cascades, from British Columbia to NV and Mexico east to NH and GA. While both *Rhus glabra* and *Rhus trilobata* are in the same family as Poison Ivy (Anacardiaceae), neither is known to cause skin irritation.

Rhus trilobata

☀ ☁ ❗ 🐝 🐦 **D 3**

Rhus trilobata Oakleaf Sumac

This large (3-6' tall by 6-10' wide), drought tolerant shrub has trilobed leaves that turn a bright red to orange color in the fall. Plants are either male or female with a bright red furry fruit produced on the female plants. It makes a nice midsize shrub for erosion control, or as a screen or hedge for a dry, sunny spot in the garden. The leaves have an odd odor when crushed and the fruit has a lemony taste when fresh, hence its other common names, Skunkbush Sumac or Lemonade Bush. Native to perennial or ephemeral streams or draws, chiefly east of the Rocky Mountains from Alberta to Mexico.

Ribes aureum

☀ ☁ ❕-💧💧 🐝 🐦 **D 3**

Ribes aureum Golden Currant

This 3-6' tall by 2-3' wide deciduous shrub produces splendid bright yellow, tubular flowers in early spring (March/April). It is one of the earliest shrubs to bloom. While it can grow in a variety of conditions, from full sun to shade and moist to moderately dry soils, it can develop an irregular, lanky growth habit in shady, dry conditions. It will grow fairly rapidly with regular irrigation. Golden Currant attracts insect pollinators and a variety of birds eat the small orange to reddish colored fruits. The currants are edible, there are no prickles on the stem, and the leaf is an attractive trilobed shape with beautiful fall colors ranging from orange to red. It occurs east of the Cascades from WA to CA, east to SD and south to NM.

☁ 💧 🐝 **D 4**

Ribes sanguineum Red-flowering Currant

Fragrant tri-lobed leaves are accompanied by pale to dark pink (and occasionally white) flower spikes in early spring. The shrub typically grows 3-5' tall by 3-4'wide. The dark black, glaucous berries are not palatable. The striking spring flowers have made this shrub popular in the horticulture industry where numerous cultivars are available. Native from British Columbia to central CA, to eastern slopes of the Cascades in WA and northern OR, east to Northern ID.

Ribes sanguineum

☀ -☀ ❕ ❗ 🐝 🐦 **D 3**

Rosa woodsii Woods' Rose

Small, pale to dark pink flowers (petals up to 1") bloom in clusters in late May. They grow 3-4' tall and spread rhizomatously to form thickets making excellent cover for wildlife with their compound leaves and recurved prickles. If space is limited, their rhizomatous habit can become a major disadvantage so care must be taken to locate accordingly. The bright red rose hips are another draw for wildlife as well as humans. With their high vitamin C content, they are often used to make teas, syrup, and jams and were used by Native Americans to cure colds, treat sores, burns, wounds, diarrhea, stomach trouble and as an eyewash (Phillips 1999). Known from eastern WA to southern CA, and eastern WI, MO and TX at moist locations in lowlands and foothills.

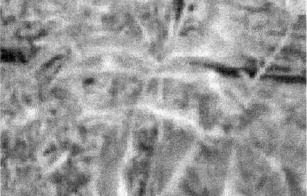

Sambucus cerulea

Sambucus cerulea **Blue Elderberry**

This deciduous shrub grows 8-12' tall by 4-6' wide and produces dense, flat-topped clusters of small, white flowers in late spring and summer. Small, fleshy, powdery blue edible berries form in late summer. The opposite branches have pinnately compound leaves with serrated margins. The interior of the stem is similar to styrofoam. It prefers plentiful water and afternoon shade to avoid scorching the leaves in hot climates. Attracts insects and birds, but not commonly browsed by deer. The fruit can be used to make wine and syrup, but berries should never be eaten before fully ripe. Prior to ripening, cyanogenic glycosides in the leaves and stems can cause cyanide poisoning (1999). Widespread species ranging from British Columbia to AZ.

Shepherdia argentea **Silver Buffaloberry**

This shrub or multi-stemmed small tree reaches 10-15 feet tall by 6-10' wide, providing a fairly dense form of silver foliage. The apetalous male and female flowers are on separate plants (dioecious), and appear prior to the leaves in early spring. Long narrow leaves are entire and covered in silver scales on both sides. Branches are opposite and may be spine-tipped. The edible reddish-yellow fruits and dense thorny growth form provide excellent bird habitat. Typical along water courses from British Columbia to southern CA on the east side of the Cascades, east to MN, and in MT east of the Rocky Mountains, but not known from WY or ID.

Sheperdia argentea (left), *Sheperdia canadensis* (right)

Shepherdia canadensis **Russet Buffaloberry**

Growing 3-12' tall by 3-6' wide, this species is slightly smaller than Silver Buffaloberry. Its leaves are blue green, often with rusty dots, and the branches are without spines. The fruit is yellow-red and bitter. Slightly more drought tolerant than *Shepherdia argentea*, it also needs well-drained soils. Native habitat includes open to wooded areas from AK to OR and throughout the US.

Symphoricarpos albus **Common Snowberry**

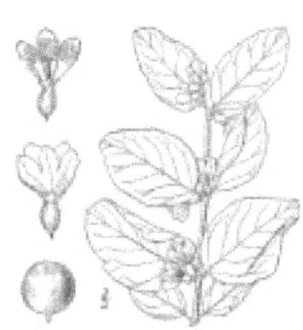

The pink to white five-lobed flowers bloom in May or June. The genus name, derived from Greek, means *syn*, together, *phorein*, to bear, and *karpos*, fruit. After flowering, white, berry-like fruits persist through summer and into winter. The total height is between 4-6' with a similar width, this shrub spreads vegetatively. Its opposite, simple leaves are entire to occasionally coarsely toothed. While moderately drought tolerant once established, it will do better with more regular water if in full sun. Native from low to mid elevations in the mountains of WA, ID, OR and MT, it often grows in thickets.

Trees

Acer grandidentatum **Big-tooth Maple**

A shrub to large tree that grows from 8-40' tall, it has opposite, 3-5 lobed leaves with toothed margins. Fall foliage varies from orange to yellow. Grows best in sun or partial shade in well-drained soils. Found from British Columbia to northern CA and east to southeast ID, MT, UT, WY and northwest CO beneath the coniferous overstory or along stream bottoms in forested areas.

Betula occidentalis **Water Birch**

This multi-stemmed tree grows 15-25' tall, producing decorative catkins or flowering structures in April and May. An excellent choice for the Rocky Mountain states, it shows more resistance to bronze birch borer than other ornamental birches. It does well on moister sites and looks excellent near a pond or stream. The male and female catkins are on the same plant, the males pendulous and 3/4" long in groups of three. The females are erect and slightly smaller. Native to the Rocky Mountain states from 3,000-9,000 feet along rivers, streams or bogs.

Celtis reticulata **Netleaf Hackberry**

This shrub to small tree grows 10-30' tall by 5-10' wide. The common name refers to the pronounced net-like veins on the underside of the leaf. Netleaf Hackberry, also known as Western Hackberry, is late to leaf out in the spring. It has inconspicuous green flowers in mid-spring followed by reddish orange berries in the fall. Remarkably hardy and long-lived despite an inhospitable landscape, Netleaf Hackberry can withstand fires after which the tree usually resprouts and becomes more shrubby. It often stands as the sole tree on a rocky, exposed hillside, providing an important source of cover for wildlife, attracting quail, chukar, deer, elk, bighorn sheep, antelope and rodents. The strong limbs and branching patterns make excellent perches and roosts for large birds such as the great horned owl. This is the only native deciduous tree in southwest ID that can tolerate xeric (dry) conditions. Native habitats include semi-desert grasslands, mountain shrub communities, riparian woodlands, and pinyon juniper forests at elevations from 500-5000'. It is widespread in the drier zones of all western states.

Juniperus occidentalis **Western Juniper**

While relatively slow growing, this freely branching evergreen tree will eventually reach 20-30' tall by 10-15' wide. Fleshy, berry-like, blue-green cones appear in the spring. The wood is very durable, often used for fence posts or pencils. Native to desert foothills and lower mountains of WA, OR, southwest ID and NV.

Larix occidentalis **Western Larch**

This large deciduous conifer can reach 150' tall. The short, soft needles grow in false whorls or clusters of 15-40 at the tips of stubby spur shoots, leaving visible the thick bark that changes to a rich cinnamon brown color with age. The needles are much broader than thick, nearly flat on the upper surface, but ridged beneath to be triangular in cross section. On younger stems the needles grow sparsely in a spiral pattern flat against the bark. Female cones are approximately 1 1/2" long. Trees turn a deep golden color in fall before leaves drop. The Western Larch, also called Tamarack, prefers a sunny location in moist, well-drained soil. Native from foothills to the midmontane, often where swampy. Its range includes southern British Columbia and east of the Cascades to northern ID, northwest MT and northeast OR.

Picea pungens

Picea pungens **Blue Spruce**

Large evergreen tree to 30' with rigid, pungent, 4-sided needles spread in all directions around the twigs, often with a bluish cast. It produces cones at least 3" long. Deer rarely browse this species. The sharp needles and dense growth provide excellent cover for birds such as chickadees, songbirds and quail, particularly when planted in clusters or small groups. Numerous cultivars are available, but the degree of "blueness" or silver-blue color is genetically determined. Native to southeast ID, WY and the southern Rocky Mountains.

Pinus edulis

E 4

Pinus edulis **Pinyon Pine**

This two-needle, 10-20 foot tall tree is slow growing and requires full sun and good drainage. The short needles are a dark green color and measure only 1-1.5" in length.
The bark is reddish brown. It is one of the most drought resistant pines. The rounded cones are 2" long and produce a highly nutritious edible nut. Pinyon pine is deer resistant. Native to higher elevations of the southwest including UT, AZ, NM, CA and TX.

E 3

Pinus monticola **Western White Pine**

The 4" long needles number 5 per fascicle (or bundle) on this distinctive pine, named Idaho's state tree in 1935. The cones are cylindrical and 6-10" long. The tree can grow very tall, the record in Idaho measuring 213'. They will grow best in sun with moist, well-drained soil. Unfortunately a disease, accidentally introduced from Europe in the early 1900s, has inflicted great damage on natural populations. It is caused by a fungus that requires two hosts for its life cycle: the white pine and a *Ribes* species (currant). Today, white pine blister rust resistant seedlings have been developed and are now being used for forestry-type plantings. For additional protection, some recommend avoiding planting any *Ribes* spp. in the vicinity (from 1916-1967 eradication efforts attempted to remove all *Ribes* from the ecosystem). *Pinus monticola* is native to moist valleys and somewhat dry slopes from sea level to more than 6,000' elevation. It ranges from southern British Columbia south to CA and western NV, and east to Idaho and western MT.

E 4

Pinus ponderosa **Ponderosa Pine**

One of the largest pines in the world and one of the most common trees in western North America. Ponderosa Pine has 3 needles per fascicle (bundle) and is the only long-needled pine in Idaho, with needles 6-10" long. The cones are 3-6" long. The yellow brown, vanilla scented jigsaw puzzle-like bark of older trees is unique. Ponderosa Pine grows in full sun in well-drained soils up to 5000' elevation. It can grow to 130' tall and is very drought tolerant.

Pinus ponderosa

D 2

Populus tremuloides **Quaking Aspen**

Groves of Quaking Aspen provide quite a scene in the fall as the small rounded leaves turn from dark green to gold, and seem to literally shimmer or tremble with a light wind. The bark is smooth and creamy white. The trees grow quickly, reaching up to 50'. They are best planted in clusters and given plenty of space, as they will spread by sending up suckers. Male and female flowers appear on separate trees and form in the spring prior to leaf set. Widespread in the mountains and tolerant of cold climates, they are more prone to disease at lower elevations. In the hot climate of southwest ID, they are best used as a fast-growing, short-lived tree, to be removed and allowed to sucker every few years. Native from AK to Labrador, south to CA, northern Mexico, and east to TN and NJ.

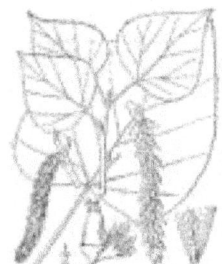 

Populus tremuloides

Populus trichocarpa

☼ ◐+ 🐦 **D 3**

Populus trichocarpa **Black Cottonwood**
(Populus balsamifera ssp. *trichocarpa)*

Largely confined to streambanks, rivers and lakeshores, this species can reach 100', but is typically smaller. Its oval leaves are glossy dark green. Black cottonwood grows quite quickly and spreads by suckers. Native from AK to Baja CA on both sides of the Cascades, and to southwest Alberta, western MT, WY and UT.

Pseudotsuga menziesii (both photos)

☼ ☁ ◐ 🐝 🐦 **E 1**

Pseudotsuga menziesii **Douglas Fir**

A wide-ranging conifer that grows up to 200' tall. The leaves are flattened, needle-like, short petiolate, and about 1 inch long. Cones are 2-4" and pendant (vs. upright like a true fir), and have distinctive bracts that resemble the tail and hind legs of a partially hidden mouse or chipmunk. Grows best in full sun on well-drained soils, but will tolerate some shade. Ranges from British Columbia to CA and east from Alberta, south to Mexico. It includes two varieties (coastal var. *menziesii*; interior var. *glauca*).

☼ ☁ ◐+ 🐝 🐦 **D 4**

Sorbus scopulina **Rocky Mountain Ash**

This shrub to small tree reaches a maximum height of 13' and can have an equally wide crown. It is distinguished from the non-native European Mountain-Ash (*S. aucuparia*) by its fine toothed leaflet margins, fewer number of leaflets (<13) with pointed tips, shrubbier growth form, and sticky winter buds with whitish hairs. Rocky Mountain Ash, like all mountain-ashes, grows best in moist, well-drained, acidic soils. The showy scarlet to orange shiny fruits are highly prized by birds, particularly cedar wax-wings. Mountain-ashes are more susceptible to disease when grown in windy, dry alkaline conditions. *Sorbus sitchensis* (Sitka Mountain Ash), native from Alaska south to northwest MT, is confined to the subalpine zone of far northern ID. It is distinguished from *S. scopulina* by its more rounded leaflet tips, glabrous calyx, and reddish hairs on the winter buds. Both native mountain ashes are similar in size and overall shape. Rocky Mountain Ash is found from AK east to the Dakotas and south to NM, CO, WY and ID.

Sorbus spp.

Scientific Name	Common Name	Flower	Grass	Shrub	Tree	Full	Partial	Shade	Dry	Low	Medium	High	Spring	Summer	Fall	Butterflies	Bees, Insects	Birds	Hummingbirds	Color	Deciduous/Evergreen	Zone
Acer glabrum	Rocky Mountain Maple			x		x	x					x	x					x	x		gr	D	3
Acer grandidentatum	Big-tooth Maple				x	x	x				x	x	x					x	x		gr	D	4
Achillea millefolium	Western Yarrow	x				x					x		x	x	x	x	x			wh	D	3
Agave parryi	Parry's Agave	x				x				x					x			x		wh	E	4
Amelanchier alnifolia	Saskatoon Serviceberry			x		x				x	x		x			x	x	x		wh	D	4
Anaphalis margaritacea	Pearly Everlasting	x				x	x			x	x			x	x	x	x			wh	D	4
Andropogon scoparium	Little Bluestem		x			x				x				x				x		bl	WI	4
Antennaria spp.	Pussytoes	x				x	x			x				x						pi/wh	SE	2
Aquilegia caerulea	Colorado Blue Columbine	x				x					x		x						x	bl/wh	D	2
Aquilegia formosa	Western Columbine	x				x					x	x	x	x					x	re, ye	D	3
Arctostaphylos uva-ursi	Kinnikinnick			x		x				x	x		x				x			pi	E	1
Artemisia cana	Silver Sagebrush			x		x			x	x					x	x		x		ye	SE	3
Artemisia frigida	Fringed Sagebrush			x		x				x				x				x		ye	SE	4
Artemisia ludoviciana	Louisiana Sage			x		x				x				x		x				ye	SE	5
Artemisia tridentata	Big Sagebrush			x		x				x	x				x	x				ye	SE	5
Aster spp.	Wild Aster	x				x				x				x		x	x			pu	D	4
Atriplex canescens	Four-wing Saltbush			x		x				x	x			x				x		NA	E	4
Balsamorhiza sagittata	Arrowleaf Balsamroot	x				x				x	x		x		x					ye	D	3
Betula occidentalis	Water Birch				x	x					x	x	x					x		NA	D	3
Bouteloua gracilis	Blue Grama		xx			x			x					x				x		gr		3
Buchloe dactyloides	Buffalograss		xx			x			x					x				x		gr		4
Camassia quamash	Blue Camas	x				x						x	x			x				bl	D	4
Celtis reticulata	Netleaf Hackberry				x	x				x	x		x			x	x			NA	D	5
Cercocarpus ledifolius	Curl-leaf Mountain Mahogany			x	x	x	x			x	x		x				x	x		ye	E	4
Cercocarpus montanus	Birch-leaf Mt Mahogany			x		x	x				x		x					x		wh	D	4
Chamaebatiaria millefolium	Fern Bush			x		x					x			x	x			x		wh	SE	4
Chrysothamnus nauseosus	Rubber Rabbitbrush			x		x				x	x				x	x	x	x	x	ye	D	3
Chrysothamnus viscidiflorus	Green Rabbitbrush			x		x				x	x				x	x				ye	E	3
Cornus stolonifera	Red-osier Dogwood			x			x	x				x		x	x			x	x	wh	D	2
Crataegus douglasii	Douglas Hawthorn			x	x	x	x				x			x	x			x	x	wh	D	3
Echinacea purpurea	Purple Coneflower	x				x	x			x	x			x	x	x				pu	D	3
Elymus elymoides	Bottlebrush Squirreltail		x			x			x					x				x		gr	E	3
Ephedra viridis	Mormon Tea			x		x				x				x		x				ye	E	5
Erigeron compositus	Cut-leaf Daisy	x				x				x				x		x				pu	SE	3
Eriogonum heracleoides	Wyeth Buckwheat	x				x					x			x		x	x	x		cr	D	4
Eriogonum niveum	Snow Buckwheat	x		x		x					x					x	x	x		wh	D	4

27

Quick Reference Guide
(Key to symbols on last page of Quick Reference Guide)

Scientific Name	Common Name	Flower	Grass	Shrub	Tree	Full	Partial	Shade	Dry	Low	Medium	High	Spring	Summer	Fall	Butterflies	Bees, Insects	Birds	Hummingbirds	Color	Deciduous/Evergreen	Zone
Eriogonum umbellatum	Sulfur Buckwheat	X				X	X		X					X		X				ye	SE	3-9
Eriophyllum lanatum	Woolly Sunflowerx	X				X	X		X					X		X				ye	D	3
Fallugia paradoxa	Apache Plume			X		X			X	X			X					X		wh-ro	D	4
Festuca idahoensis	Idaho Fescue		X			X	X			X	X		X					X		bl	E	4
Festuca ovina	Sheep Fescue		XX			X	X		X	X	X		X					X		gr	Wl	5
Gaillardia aristata	Blanket Flower	X				X	X			X	X			X	X	X				ye,re	D	2
Geranium viscosissimum	Sticky Geranium	X				X	X			X	X		X	X		X		X	X	pi-pu	D	2
Geum triflorum	Prairie Smoke	X				X	X				X		X			X				pi-pu	D	2
Hesperaloe parviflora	Texas Red Yucca	X		X		X	X		X					X					X	re	E	5
Ipomopsis or *Gilia aggregata*	Scarlet Gilia	X				X	X		X					X					X	re	D	2
Juniperus occidentalis	Western Juniper				X	X			X	X			X				X	X		NA	E	5
Krascheninnikovia (Ceratoides) lanata	Winterfat		X			X			X				X					X		NA	E	3
Larix occidentalis	Western Larch				X	X					X	X	X				X	X		NA	D	3
Leymus cinereus	Great Basin Wildrye		X			X			X				X					X		gr	Wl	3
Linum perenne	Wild Blue Flax	X				X				X	X		X	X						bl	D	4
Lupinus argenteus	Silver Lupine	X				X	X			X	X			X		X				bl-wh	D	5
Mahonia repens	Creeping Oregon Grape			X			X	X	X	X			X			X				ye	E	4
Oenothera missouriensis	Missouri Evening Primrose	X				X				X	X			X	X	X	X			ye	D	4
Opuntia spp.	Prickly Pear Cactus	X				X			X					X			X	X		ye,or, re,pi	E	5
Oryzopsis hymenoides	Indian Ricegrass		X			X			X				X					X		bl	Wl	5-
Penstemon angustifolius	Pagoda Penstemon	X				X			X					X		X			X	bl	D	4
Penstemon barbatus	Scarlet Bugler	X				X			X					X	X				X	re	D	4
Penstemon cyaneus	Dark Blue Penstemon	X				X			X				X	X		X			X	**bl**-pu	D	5
Penstemon deustus	Hot Rock Penstemon	X				X				X	X		X	X		X				cr	D	5
Penstemon eatonii	Firecracker Penstemon	X				X			X				X			X			X	re	D	4
Penstemon fruticosus	Shrubby Penstemon	X				X				X	X		X			X			X	bl-pu	SE	5
Penstemon palmeri	Palmer Penstemon	X				X			X	X			X	X					X	pi	SE	4
Penstemon pinifolius	Pine-leaf Penstemon	X				X			X					X	X	X			X	re, ye	E	3-
Penstemon rydbergii	Rydberg's Penstemon	X				X	X				X		X			X			X	bl-pu	D	2
Penstemon speciosus	Showy Penstemon	X				X	X		X	X			X			X		X	X	pu	D	5
Penstemon strictus	Rocky Mt Penstemon	X				X			X	X			X			X			X	bl-pu	D	4
Penstemon venustus	Lovely Penstemon	X				X	X				X		X			X		X	X	pu	D	5
Penstemon whippleanus	Whipple's Penstemon	X					X				X			X	X	X				pu-bl	D	3
Petalostemon purpureum	Prairie Clover	X				X			X					X		X	X			pu	D	3
Philadelphus lewisii	Mockorange, Syringa			X		X	X		X	X			X					X		wh	D	5

Quick Reference Guide
(Key to symbols on last page of Quick Reference Guide)

Scientific Name	Common Name	Flower	Grass	Shrub	Tree	Full	Partial	Shade	Dry	Low	Medium	High	Spring	Summer	Fall	Butterflies	Bees, Insects	Birds	Hummingbirds	Color	Deciduous/Evergreen	Zone
Physocarpus malvaceus	Ninebark			x			x	x	x				x			x				wh	D	3
Picea pungens	Blue Spruce				x	x	x				x		x					x	x	NA	E	3
Pinus monticola	Western White Pine				x	x	x				x	x	x					x	x	NA	E	3
Pinus ponderosa	Ponderosa Pine				x	x			x	x			x					x	x	NA	E	4
Populus tremuloides	Quaking Aspen				x	x	x					x	x						x	NA	D	2
Populus trichocarpa	Black Cottonwood				x	x						x	x					x	x	NA	D	3
Potentilla fruticosa	Shrubby Cinquefoil			x			x		x				x	x	x	x				ye	D	3
Prunus emarginata	Bitter Cherry			x		x	x			x	x		x					x	x	wh	D	4
Prunus virginiana	Chokecherry			x	x	x	x				x		x				x	x	x	wh	D	3
Pseudoroegneria spicata	Bluebunch Wheatgrass		x			x			x				x						x	gr	WI	4
Pseudotsuga menziesii	Douglas Fir				x	x	x				x		x					x	x	NA	E	1
Purshia tridentata	Antelope Bitterbrush			x		x			x	x			x						x	ye	SE	4
Rhus glabra	Smooth Sumac			x		x	x		x	x			x						x	wh	D	4
Rhus trilobata	Oakleaf Sumac			x		x	x		x	x			x						x	ye	D	3
Ribes aureum	Golden Currant			x		x				x	x	x	x					x	x	ye	D	3
Ribes sanguineum	Red-flowering Currant			x			x				x		x						x	pi-re	D	4
Rosa woodsii	Woods' Rose			x		x	x	x	x	x			x					x	x	pi	D	3
Sambucus caerulea	Blue Elderberry			x		x	x					x		x				x	x	wh	D	3
Shepherdia argentea	Silver Buffaloberry			x			x				x	x	x					x	x	ye	D	3
Shepherdia canadensis	Russet Buffaloberry			x		x	x		x	x			x						x	ye	D	2
Solidago spp.	Goldenrod	x				x					x			x	x	x	x	x	x	ye	D	1
Sorbus scopulina	Rocky Mountain Ash				x	x	x				x		x					x	x	wh	D	4
Sphaeralcea ambigua	Desert Globemallow	x				x					x		x	x		x				or-re	D	6
Sphaeralcea grossulariifolia	Gooseberry-leaf Globemallow	x				x			x	x			x	x	x	x				or-re	D	4
Sphaeralcea munroana	Orange Globemallow	x					x	x	x	x			x	x	x	x				re-or	D	4
Sporobolus cryptandrus	Sand Dropseed		x			x			x					x					x	gr	WI	4
Stanleya pinnata	Prince's Plume	x				x			x				x	x		x				ye	D	4
Symphoricarpos albus	Common Snowberry			x			x	x	x				x					x	x	pi-wh	D	3
Yucca glauca	Narrowleaf Yucca	x		x		x					x		x			x				wh-cr	E	3

KEY FOR QUICK REFERENCE GUIDE

PLANT FORM
xx=lawn alternative

COLORS
bl=blue ye=yellow
cr=cream pu=purple
or=orange **bl**=dark blue
pi=pink cr-ye=varies btwn 2 colors
re=red cr, ye=includes both colors
wh=white

D OR E
D=Deciduous
E=Evergreen
WI=Winter Interest
SE=Semi-evergreen
NA=flowers inconspicuous

Landscaping to Reduce the Risk of Wild Fires

The following information is a brief introduction to "Firewise" concepts in relation to the native plants presented in this manual. For more comprehensive information about creating a "Firewise Landscape," consult your local BLM, Forest Service Office, or fire department.

If your property is adjacent to the foothills, or other dry wildlands, assess whether your landscape design will help or hinder flames from reaching your home. The flammability of the home's exterior, façade and roof (brick, stucco, concrete vs. wood, etc.) may play the biggest role in the home's risk, but additional issues must be considered as well. These include the amount of flammable material surrounding the home, the property's slope, location and prevailing winds.

To reduce flammable material and conserve water at the same time, create landscaping zones around your home. The first zone should be a 30-foot perimeter immediately surrounding the structure that should receive the highest amount of irrigation to stay green during the hottest months. Fire officials term this "defensible space" and recommend that this 30 feet be relatively clear so that they can access the area and maneuver easily. Trees should be routinely cleaned of dead branches and trimmed back from the roof. All dried plant material, leaves etc., should be swept away to reduce potential sources of fuel.

Anything beyond the 30' perimeter may still have the potential to ignite the house depending on the heat energy of the fire. The heat energy will determine the radiant energy, flame length and the creation of firebrands, which can directly ignite the house. Heat energy is defined as "the amount, arrangement and rate of combustion of the vegetative fuels" (www.firewise.org). The arrangement of the plants can play a crucial role. For example, a hedge of junipers on a property line that leads up to the corner of a house will form a direct line like a fuse to ignite the home. Breaking up clumps or hedges of flammable plant material will help break the momentum of the fire. The rate of combustion of vegetative fuels will decrease the more water that plants retain, and increase if the plants are aromatic or contains oils. Salt content will decrease the rate of combustion.

Additional factors that determine combustion rates are the plants height and density. A shorter, squatter stature will not burn as rapidly as a tall one. Plants with an open branching pattern will not burn as fast as those with a tight dense pattern, like a juniper (Dennis 1999). Many conifers such as cypress, cedar, juniper, and pine tend to be highly flammable due to their high oil content and small leaf size, but limbing them up 10' may reduce their chances of ignition (Wilders 2002). A better choice is the broadleaf deciduous trees such as maple, poplar, willows, etc. Examples of highly combustible plants, or pyrophytes, are listed in the table below, along with some alternatives.

The alternatives are not in any way fireproof. They are fire retardant, meaning they may slow rather than accelerate the rate of the fire.

Highly Combustible Plants	Alternatives
Bold means ***extremely*** combustible	(Same cultural requirements and similar either in size or form)
SHRUBS AND GROUNDCOVERS	
Yarrow (*Achillea* spp.) (aromatic, and may dry out in summer)	Lewis Flax *(Linum lewisii)*, Evening Primrose *(Oenothera* spp.)
Algerian Ivy (*Hedera canariensis*)	Prickly Pear Cactus (*Opuntia* spp.)
Sagebrush (*Artemisia* spp.) (aromatic)	Saltbush (*Atriplex* spp.), Red Yucca (*Hesperaloe parviflora*)
Brooms *(Genista)*	Kinnikinnick (*Arctostaphylos uva-ursi*), Buckwheat (*Eriogonum* spp.)
Herbs (Lavender, Rosemary, etc.)	Buckwheat (*Eriogonum* spp.), Apache Plume *(Fallugia paradoxa)*
Juniper *(Juniperus* spp.)	Oregon Grape (*Mahonia* spp.), Wild Rose (*Rosa woodsii*), Oakleaf Sumac (*Rhus trilobata*), Currant (*Ribes* spp.), Mockorange (*Philadelphus lewisii*)
Santolina (*Santolina* spp.)	Narrowleaf Yucca (*Yucca glauca*), Silver Lupine (*Lupinus argenteus*)
GRASSES	
Bamboo spp. (*Phyllostachys, Bambusa*)	Bluebunch Wheatgrass *(Pseudoroegneria spicata)*, Sand Dropseed *(Sporobolus cryptandrus)*, Buffalo Grass (*Buchloe dactyloides)*, Sandberg Bluegrass *(Poa secunda)*
Maiden Grass/Silver Grass (*Miscanthus*)	
Fountain Grass (*Pennisetum*)	

Some of the plants listed here were provided by FireSafe Council of Nevada County or by Colorado State University's FireWise Plant Materials No. 6.305.

Additional alternatives, particularly for the 30' perimeter immediately around the home, are succulents such as Hens and Chicks *(Sempervivum spp.)*, cactus, and sedum. They can retain water and are low-growing, preventing the formation of a "ladder" for the fire to reach your home. Colorado State University Cooperative Extension (1999) has written a brochure on Firewise Plant Material that includes a much longer list of fire retardant plants developed by Phil Hoefer of the Forest Service.
The brochure is No 6.305 of the Natural Resource Series or it can be accessed on line at
http://www.co.pueblo.co.us/fire/plants.pdf

Additional notes: While swimming pools or ponds consume a great deal of water, they can be helpful in fire prevention when positioned appropriately. Because the fire will move most rapidly uphill they are most effective when placed on the downward slope to provide a barrier between the pool and the home. The surrounding hardscape, (walls, steps, etc.) should be constructed to allow firemen and fire trucks access to the water. Wooden trellises, decks, and patios can become a bridge for flames to reach your home: try to use masonry, or wood with a 2-hour fire-resistive rating as specified in the UBC. Fencing: single strand wire fence or masonry are alternatives to the more flammable post and rail. Keep wood piles well away from the home's perimeter. Clean rooftops and gutters of debris, particularly pine needles and other dried plant material.

From the *The Xeriscape Flower Gardener* (Knopf 1991).
Xeriscape comes from the word *xeri*, which means dry, and scape, which means vista.

The Seven Principles of Xeriscape

1) **Plant and Design** comprehensively from the beginning.

2) **Create practical turf areas** of manageable sizes, shapes, and appropriate grasses.

3) **Use appropriate plants and zone the landscape** according to the water needs of the plants.

4) **Consider improving the soil** with organic matter like compost or manure.

5) **Consider using mulches** such as wood chips.

6) **Irrigate efficiently** with properly designed systems (including hose-end equipment) and by applying the right amount of water at the right time.

7) **Maintain the landscape appropriately** by mowing, pruning, and fertilizing properly.

Site Specific Recommendations

! Indicates the conditions are not ideal (refer to plant guide and severity of site).

HOT DRY EXPOSURE
Wildflowers
Agave parryi
Anaphalis margaritacea
Erigeron compositus
Hesperaloe parviflora
Ipomopsis aggregata
Linum perenne
Oenothera missouriensis
Opuntia spp.
Penstemon angustifolius
Pensetmon barbatus
Penstemon cyaneus
Penstemon eatonii
Penstemon palmeri
Penstemon pinifolius
Petalostemon purpureum
Sphaeralcea spp.
Sphaeralcea munroana
Stanleya pinnata
Yucca glauca
Grasses
Bouteloua gracilis
Buchloe dactyloides
Elymus elymoides
Festuca ovina
Leymus cinereus
Oryzopsis hymenoides
Pseudoroegneria spicata
Sporobolus cryptandrus

Shrubs
Chrysothamnus spp.
Artemisia cana
Artemisia tridentata
Atriplex canescens
Cercocarpus ledifolius

(shrubs continued)
Chamaebatiaria millefolium
Ephedra spp.
Fallugia paradoxa
Juniperus occidentalis
Krascheninnikovia lanata
Purshia tridentata
Rhus trilobata
Rosa woodsii
Shepherdia canadensis

Trees
Celtis reticulata
Pinus ponderosa
Pinus edulis

DRY SHADE
Grasses
Festuca ovina

Shrubs
Arctostaphylos uva-ursi
Mahonia repens
Philadelphus lewisii!
Physocarpus malvaceus!
Symphoricarpos albus!

MOIST SHADE
Wildflowers
Aquilegia caerulea
Aquilegia formosa
Geranium viscossisimum

Grasses
Festuca idahoensis!

(moist shade cont.)
Shrubs
Acer glabrum
Amelanchier alnifolia!
Cornus stolonifera
Ribes sanguineum!

Trees
Acer grandidentaum
Picea pungens!
Populus tremuloides
Pseudotsuga menziesii

COLORFUL FALL FOLIAGE
Grasses
Festuca spp.
Leymus cinereus

Shrubs
Acer glabrum
Amelanchier alnifolia
Physocarpus malvaceus
Rhus trilobata
Ribes aureum

Trees
Acer grandidentatum
Larix occidentalis
Populus tremuloides
Populus trichocarpa
Sorbus scopulina

INVASIVE ORNAMENTALS: DO NOT PLANT
(Plants that escape cultivation, become weedy, and out compete native plants)

Centaurea cyanus Bachelor Buttons/Cornflower*
Centaurea maculosa Spotted Knapweed
Centaurea pratensis Meadow Knapweed
Cichorium intybus Chicory
Cytisus scoparius Scotch Broom*
Delospermum Ice Plant (highly invasive in CA)*
Elaeagnus augustifolia Russian-Olive*
Euphorbia cyaparissias Cypress Spurge
Euphorbia myrsinites Myrtle Spurge*
Hesperis matronalis Dame's Rocket
Hieracium aurantiacum Orange Hawkweed
Hyoscyamus niger Black Henbane
Hypericum perforatum St. Johnswort*
Lepidium latifolium Perennial Pepperweed
Linaria vulgaris Yellow toadflax
Lythrum salicari,L. virgatum Purple Loosestrife*
Potentilla recta Sulfur Cinquefoil*
Saponaria officinalis Bouncingbet*
Tamarix parviflora, T. ramosissima Saltcedar

*Widely available at nurseries in Boise, ID and surrounding vicinity at time of publication

More Reasons to Use Native Plants and Reduce Turfgrass

From the National Wildlife Federation

- 30 percent of water consumed on the East Coast goes to watering lawns; 60 percent on the West Coast. (*Redesigning the American Lawn*)

- A 1000 square foot lawn requires 10,000 gallons of water per summer to maintain a "green" look. (*U.S. News and World Report*, 10/28/96)

- Eighteen percent of municipal solid waste collected is composed of organic yard waste. This is 31 million tons a year. (EPA's *Consumer Handbook for Reducing Solid Waste*)

- The average suburban lawn is deluged with ten times as much chemical pesticide per acre as farmland. (Yale Graduate Study)

- In the Mississippi watershed, a study found that 44 percent of nitrogen and 28 percent of phosphorous applied ends up washed into the Mississippi River, and eventually the Gulf of Mexico, causing significant environmental problems.

- A lawn mower emits as much hydrocarbon in one hour as a typical auto driven 50 miles. One hour of chain saw operation equates to the emissions of an auto driven 200 miles. (National Vehicle and Fuel Emissions Lab, Ann Arbor)

- Per hour of operation, a lawn mower emits 10-12 times as much hydrocarbon as a typical auto; a string trimmer emits 21 times more and a leaf blower 34 times more.

- A typical four-stroke lawnmower spends 40 hour per year – the equivalent of a one-week vacation – mowing the lawn.

- Harmful invasive plants out-compete native plants, reducing biodiversity and habitat value. For example, kudzu now covers more than 7 million acres in the U.S., mostly in the Southeast. (USFWS)

- It costs an average of $700 per acre per year to maintain a lawn; a wildflower meadow costs $30/acre.

Native and Drought-Tolerant Landscaping Sources

Compiled by the Pahove Chapter, Idaho Native Plant Society. Inclusion on this list is not necessarily an endorsement by INPS or others involved in the development of this publication.

Buffalo-Berry Farm
P.O. Box 749
Lake Fork, ID 83635
(208) 634-3062

Clifty View Nursery
Rt. 1, Box 509
Bonners Ferry, ID 83805
(208) 267-7129

Cly Robbins Seed Co.
P.0. Box 2366
Castro Valley, CA 94546

Cusheon Creek Nursery
175 Stewart Rd.
Salt Spring Island , BC V8K 2C4 Canada
E-mail: cusheoncreek@saltspring.com
http://www.com/~amdigest/cusheon.htm

Earthly Goods
620 East Main Street
New Albany, IN 47150
24-hour phone/fax: (812) 944-2903
(812) 944-3283   **http://www.earthlygoods.com**

Freshwater Farms/North Coast Native Seed Bank
5851 Myrtle Avenue
Eureka, CA 95503-9510 USA
(800) 200-8969 Fax: (707) 442-2490
E-mail: r.storre@worldnet.att.net
http://www.freshwaterfarms.com/

Forest Farm
990 Tetherow Rd.
Williams, OR 97544
(541) 846-6963
http://www.forestfarm.com

Granite Seed
1697 West 2100 North
Lehi, UT 84043
(801) 768-4422 or 531-1456

Great Basin Native Plants
75 West 300 South
Holden, UT 84636
(801) 768-4422
E-mail: Gbn@gbasin.com

High Altitude Gardens
P.O. Box 4238
Ketchum, ID 83340
(800) 874-7333
http://www.seedsave.org/

High Country Gardens
2902 Rufina Street
Santa Fe, NM 87505
1-800-925-9387
http://www.highcountrygardens.com

Idaho State Nursery
University of Idaho
Moscow, ID 83843
(208) 885-7023

Jacklin Seed Co.
17300 Jacklin Ave.
Post Falls, ID

Jayker Wholesale Nursery
801 E. Beacon Light Road
Eagle, ID 83616
(208) 939-9639 or 939-0014

Lawyer Nursery
Rt. 2, Box 95
Plains, MT 59859
(406) 826-3881

Maple Leaf Industries, Inc.
Box 496
Ephraim, UT 84627
(801) 283-4701

Maxwelton Valley Gardens
3443 E. French Road
Clinton, WA 98236 USA
(360) 579-1770 Fax: (360) 579-1496
http://www.whidbey.com/mvg/

Mountain States Wholesale Nursery
P.O. Box 2500
Litchfield Park, Arizona 85340-2500
(623) 247-8509   (800) 840-8509
http://www.mswn.com/index2.htm

Moss Greenhouses
269 South 100 East
Jerome, ID 83338
(208) 324-8325

Native Seed Foundation
Star Route
Moyie Springs, ID   83845
(208) 267-7938

Native Origins Nursery
1129 Water Street
Raymond, WA 98577 USA
(360) 942-0027 Fax: (360) 942-6060
E-mail: maryann@willapabay.org

Natives Northwest
190 Aldrich Rd.
Mossyrock, WA 98564 USA
(360) 983-3138 Fax: (360) 491-6904

Nature's Enhancement
2980 Eastside Highway
Stevensville, MT 59870
(406) 777-3560

North American Rock Garden Society
P.O Box 67
Millwood, NY 10546 USA
http://www.mobot.org/NARGS/

Plants of the Southwest
1812 Second Street
Santa Fe, NM 87501
http://www.plantsofthesouthwest.com

Plants of the Wild
Division of Palouse Seed
P.O. Box 866
Tekoa, WA 99033
(509) 284-2848

Plato Nursery
HCR 60, Box 1
Bonners Ferry, ID 83805
(208) 267-3742

Progressive Plants
9180 South Wasatch Blvd
Sandy, UT 84093
(801) 942-7333

Rainier Seeds, Inc.
1404 Fourth St.
Davenport, WA 99122
(509) 725-1235 (800) 828-8873

Sevenoaks Native Nursery
2320 NW Huntington Drive
Corvallis, OR 97330 USA
Phone: 541-745-5540 Fax: 541-745-5540

Siskiyou Rare Plant Nursery
2825 Cummings Road
Medford, OR 97501
http://www.srpn.net

Sound Native Plants
PO Box 10155
Olympia, WA 98502 USA
(360) 866-1046 Fax: (360) 943-7026

Stevenson Intermountain Seed
P.O. Box 2
Ephraim, UT 84627
(801) 283-6639

Sun Mountain Native Seeds
Rt. 1
Eagle, ID 83616
(208) 286-7004

Wildland Nursery
550 North Highway 89
Joseph, UT 84739
http://www.wildlandnursery.com/

Wind River Seed
Route 1, Box 97
Manderson, WY 82432
(307) 568-3361

Wood's Native Plants
5740 Berry Drive
Parkdale, OR 97041 USA
(503) 352-7497

Literature Cited

Dennis, F. C. 1999. "Forestry: FireWise Plant Material No. 6.305," Natural Resources Series, Colorado State University Cooperative Extension. **http://www.co.pueblo.co.us/fire/plants.pdf**

Denver Water. 1998. *Xeriscape Plant Guide*. American Water Works Association. Fulcrum Publishing.

Hitchcock, C. L. and Cronquist, A. 2001. *Flora of the Pacific Northwest: An Illustrated Manual*. University Of Washington Press, Seattle.

Knopf, J. 1991. *The Xeriscape Flower Gardener*. Johnson Books, Boulder, CO.

Kruckeberg, A. 1993. *Gardening with Native Plants of the Pacific Northwest: An Illustrated Guide*. University of Washington Press, Seattle.

Mozingo, H. 1987. *Shrubs of the Great Basin*. University of Nevada Press, Las Vegas.

Nold, R. 1999. *Penstemons*. Timber Press, Portland, OR.

Ogle, D.G., compiler. 1997. *Plant Guide Handbook. Natural Resource Conservation Service*, Boise, ID. No page numbers.

O'Keefe, J. 1992. *Water-Conserving Gardens and Landscapes*. Storey Publishing, Pownal, Vermont.

Phillips, W. H. 1998. *Canyon Country Wildflowers*. Falcon Publishing Co, Inc., Helena, MT.

Phillips, W. H. 1999. *Central Rocky Mountain Wildflowers*. Globe Pequot Press, Guilford, Connecticut.

Phillips, W. H. 2003. *Plants of the Lewis and Clark Expedition*. Mountain Press Publishing Company, Missoula, MT.

Strickler, D. 1997. *Northwest Penstemons*. Flower Press, Columbia Falls, MT.

www.firewise.org

United States Department of Agriculture, Natural Resources Conservation Service PLANTS Database. August 2003. **http://plants.usda.gov/index.html**

Recommended Reading by Topic and Sources of Additional Information

LANDSCAPING

Bormann, H., Balmori, D. and Geballe, G. 2001. *Redesigning the American Lawn: A Search for Environmental Harmony, Second Edition.* Yale University Press, New Haven, CT.

Denver Water. 1998. *Xeriscape Plant Guide.* American Water Works Association. Fulcrum Publishing.

Knopf, J. 1991. *The Xeriscape Flower Gardener.* Johnson Books, Boulder, CO.

Kruckeberg, A. 1993. *Gardening with Native Plants of the Pacific Northwest: An Illustrated Guide:* University of Washington Press, Seattle.

Mee, W., Barnes, J., Sutton, R., Kjelgren, R., Cerny, T. and Johnson, C. 2003. *Water Wise: Native Plants for Intermountain Landscapes.* Utah State University Press, Logan, UT.

O'Keefe, J. 1992. *Water-Conserving Gardens and Landscapes.* Storey Publishing, Pownal, Vermont, 1992.

REFERENCE GUIDES

Hitchcock, C. L. and Cronquist, A. 2001. *Flora of the Pacific Northwest: An Illustrated Manual.* University Of Washington Press, Seattle.

Mozingo, H. 1987. *Shrubs of the Great Basin.* University of Nevada Press, Las Vegas.

Nold, R. 1999. *Penstemons.* Timber Press, Portland.

Phillips, W. H. 1998. *Canyon Country Wildflowers.* Falcon Publishing Co, Inc., Helena, MT.

Phillips, W. H. 1999. *Central Rocky Mountain Wildflowers.* Globe Pequot Press, Guilford, Connecticut.

Phillips, W. H. 2003. *Plants of the Lewis and Clark Expedition.* Mountain Press Publishing Company, Missoula, MT.

Strickler, D. 1997. *Northwest Penstemons.* Flower Press, Columbia Falls, MT.

Taylor, R. J. and Ort, K. 2003. *Sagebrush Country: A Wildlife Sanctuary.* Mountain Press Publishing Company, Missoula, Montana.

LANDSCAPING FOR WILDLIFE

Adams, G. M. 1998. *Birdscaping Your Garden: A Practical Guide to Backyard Birds and the Plants That Attract Them.* Rodale Press, Emmaus, PA.

Ellis, B. 1997. *Taylor's Weekend Gardening Guide to Attracting Birds and Butterflies: How to Plant a Backyard Habitat to Attract Hummingbirds and Other Winged Wildlife.* Houghton Mifflin Co., Boston.

Pyle, R. M. 1974. *Watching Washington Butterflies: An Interpretive Guide to the State's 134 Species, Including Most of the Butterflies of Oregon, Idaho and British Columbia.* Seattle Audobon Society, Seattle.

Xerces Society. Smithsonian Institute. Sierra Club Books. 1998. *Butterfly Gardening: Creating Summer Magic in Your Garden, 2nd Edition.* Sierra Club Books, San Francisco.

USEFUL ORGANIZATIONS AND WEBSITES

Drip Irrigation Source (offers a free catalogue with instructions) **http://www.dripworksusa.com/**

Drip Irrigation Solutions from Netafim USA (uses thick tubing to prevent clogs) **http://www.netafim-usa.com/**

Drip Store Online (offers pre-packaged kits and tutorials) **http://www.dripirrigation.com/**

A Source Book on Natural Landscaping for Public Officials **http://www.epa.gov/greenacres/toolkit/about.html**

Center for Invasive Plant Management **http://www.weedcenter.org/info/info.html**

Idaho Native Plant Society **www.idahonativeplants.org**

Forest Service http://www.fs.fed.us/psw/publications/documents/ gtr-050/accessories.html

National Wildlife Federation **www.nwf.org**

Native Plant Network **www.nativeplantnetwork.org**

NRCS (Natural Resources Conservation Service) PLANTS Database **http://plants.usda.gov/index.html**

S.A.L.T: Smaller American Lawns Today **http://arboretum.conncoll.edu/salt/salt.html**

"Sustainable Landscaping: The Hidden Impacts of Gardens" **http://www.epa.gov/greenacres/smithsonian.pdf**

U.S. Department of Agriculture, Forest Service, Rocky Mountain Research Station, Fire Sciences Laboratory (August 2003). Fire Effects Information System: **http://www.fs.fed.us/database/feis/**

U.S. Environmental Protection Agency: Green Landscaping with Native Plants **http://www.epa.gov/greenacres/**

U.S. Fire Administration Site http://www.usfa.fema.gov/public/factsheets/landscape.shtm

Wild Ones-Natural Landscapers, Ltd. **www.for-wild.org**

Wilders, Tineke. (June 7, 2002). "California Gardens: prepare for fire season with low-fuel plants" North County Times. **http://www.nctimes.net/news/2002/20020607/92231.html**

Photo Credits

WILDFLOWERS

Anaphalis margaritacea Ann DeBolt

Aquilegia caerulea Hilary Parkinson

Aster spp. Ann DeBolt

Balsamorhiza sagittata Hilary Parkinson

Camassia quamash Ann DeBolt

Erigeron compositus Gary A. Monroe @ USDA-NRCS PLANTS Database.

Eriogonum heracleoides Ann DeBolt

Eriogonum umbellatum with dark yellow flowers (left), *E. heracleoides* with creamy flowers (right) Ann DeBolt.

Eriophyllum lanatum Gary A. Monroe @ USDA-NRCS PLANTS Database.

Geum triflorum in bud (left), seed head (right) Gary A. Monroe @ USDA-NRCS PLANTS Database.

Hesperaloe parviflora foliage (left), summer flowers (right) J.S. Peterson @ USDA-NRCS PLANTS Database.

Ipomopsis aggregata Ann DeBolt

Linum perenne Brother Alfred Brousseau @ USDA-NRCS PLANTS Database.

Lupinus argenteus Ann DeBolt

Opuntia spp. W.L. Wagner @ USDA-NRCS PLANTS Database.

Penstemon eatonii Hilary Parkinson

Penstemon palmeri Hilary Parkinson

Penstemon pinifolius close-up (left), en masse at 3+ yrs (right) Ann DeBolt.

Penstemon rydbergii James L. Reveal @ USDA-NRCS PLANTS Database.

Penstemon speciosus Brother Alfred Brousseau @ USDA-NRCS PLANTS Database.

Petalostemon purpureum W.L. Wagner (left); Larry Allain (right) @ USDA-NRCS PLANTS Database.

Sphaeralcea spp. Hilary Parkinson

Stanleya pinnata Brother Alfred Brousseau @ USDA-NRCS PLANTS Database.

Yucca glauca Clarence A. Rechenthin @ USDA-NRCS PLANTS Database.

GRASSES

Achnatherum hymenoides Gary A. Monroe @ USDA-NRCS PLANTS Database.

Achnatherum hymenoides USDA-NRCS PLANTS Database / Britton, N.L., and A. Brown. 1913. *Illustrated flora of the northern states and Canada.* Vol. 1: 174.

Andropogon scoparium (left) USDA-NRCS PLANTS Database / Hitchcock, A.S. (rev. A. Chase). 1950. *Manual of the grasses of the United States.* USDA Misc. Publ. No. 200. Washington, DC.

Bouteloua gracilis (right) USDA-NRCS PLANTS Database / Hitchcock, A.S. (rev. A. Chase). 1950. *Manual of the grasses of the United States.* USDA Misc. Publ. No. 200. Washington, DC.

Buchloe dactyloides (left), USDA-NRCS PLANTS Database / Britton, N.L., and A. Brown. 1913. *Illustrated flora of the northern states and Canada.* Vol. 1: 231.

Elymus elymoides (right) USDA-NRCS PLANTS Database / Hitchcock, A.S. (rev. A. Chase). 1950. *Manual of the grasses of the United States.* USDA Misc. Publ. No. 200. Washington, DC.

Festuca idahoensis (left) USDA-NRCS PLANTS Database: Hitchcock, A.S. (rev. A. Chase). 1950. *Manual of the grasses of the United States.* USDA Misc. Publ. No. 200. Washington, DC.

Festuca ovina (right) USDA-NRCS PLANTS Database / Britton, N.L., and A. Brown. 1913. *Illustrated flora of the northern states and Canada.* Vol. 1: 271.

Leymus cinereus early June (left), same species in late winter (right) Hilary Parkinson.

Pseudoroegneria spicata (left) USDA-NRCS PLANTS Database / Hitchcock, A.S. (rev. A. Chase). 1950. *Manual of the grasses of the United States.* USDA Misc. Publ. No. 200. Washington, DC.

Sporobolus cryptandrus (right) USDA-NRCS PLANTS Database / Hitchcock, A.S. (rev. A. Chase). 1950. *Manual of the grasses of the United States.* USDA Misc. Publ. No. 200. Washington, DC.

SHRUBS

Acer glabrum USDA-NRCS PLANTS Database / Britton, N.L., and A. Brown. 1913. *Illustrated flora of the northern states and Canada.* Vol. 2: 497.

Amelanchier alnifolia Hilary Parkinson

Arctostaphylos uva-ursi over rock wall (left), close up of foliage and fruit (right) Ann DeBolt.

Artemisia cana Ann DeBolt

Artemisia frigida Hilary Parkinson

Atriplex canescens (in background), Ann DeBolt

Cercocarpus ledifolius (left) Hilary Parkinson, closeup of leaves (right) Ann DeBolt.

Chamaebatiaria millefolium Ann DeBolt

Crataegus douglasii USDA-NRCS PLANTS Database / Britton, N.L., and A. Brown. 1913. *Illustrated flora of the northern states and Canada*. Vol. 2: 321.

Ephedra viridis USDA-NRCS PLANTS Database

Fallugia paradoxa W.L. Wagner @ USDA-NRCS PLANTS Database (both).

Krascheninnikovia (Ceratoides) lanata (left) Gary A. Monroe @ USDA-NRCS PLANTS Database.

Krascheninnikovia (Ceratoides) lanata (right) Britton, N.L., and A. Brown. USDA-NRCS PLANTS Database, 1913. *Illustrated flora of the northern states and Canada*. Vol. 2: 20. Courtesy of Kentucky Native Plant Society.

Philadelphus lewisii Ann DeBolt

Potentilla fruticosa Ann DeBolt

Prunus emarginata in flower (left), in fruit (right) Brother Alfred Brousseau @ USDA-NRCS PLANTS Database.

Purshia tridentata Brother Alfred Brousseau @ USDA-NRCS PLANTS Database.

Rhus glabra F. Larry Allain @ USDA-NRCS PLANTS Database.

Rhus glabra USDA-NRCS PLANTS Database / Herman, D.E. et al. 1996. *North Dakota tree handbook*. USDA NRCS ND State Soil Conservation Committee; NDSU Extension and Western Area Power Admin., Bismarck, ND.

Rhus trilobata W.L. Wagner. @ USDA-NRCS PLANTS Database.

Ribes aureum Hilary Parkinson

Ribes sanguineum Brother Alfred Brousseau @ USDA-NRCS PLANTS Database.

Sambucus cerulea flowers (left) and fruit (right) J.S. Peterson @ USDA-NRCS PLANTS Database .

Shepherdia argentea Britton, N.L., and A. Brown. USDA-NRCS PLANTS Database, 1913. *Illustrated flora of the northern states and Canada*. Vol. 2: 577. Courtesy of Kentucky Native Plant Society.

Shepherdia canadensis Britton, N.L., and A. Brown. 1913. *Illustrated flora of the northern states and Canada*. Vol. 2: 576. Courtesy of Kentucky Native Plant Society.

Symphoricarpos albus Britton, N.L., and A. Brown. 1913. *Illustrated flora of the northern states and Canada*. Vol. 3: 276. Courtesy of Kentucky Native Plant Society.

TREES

Picea pungens USDA-NRCS PLANTS Database / Herman, D.E. et al. 1996. *North Dakota tree handbook*. USDA NRCS ND State Soil Conservation Committee; NDSU Extension and Western Area Power Admin., Bismarck, ND.

Pinus edulis J.S. Peterson @ USDA-NRCS PLANTS Database.

Pinus ponderosa USDA-NRCS PLANTS Database / Herman, D.E. et al. 1996. *North Dakota tree handbook*. USDA NRCS ND State Soil Conservation Committee; NDSU Extension and Western Area Power Admin., Bismarck, ND.

Populus tremuloides Britton, N.L., and A. Brown. 1913. *Illustrated flora of the northern states and Canada*. Vol. 1: 590. Courtesy of Kentucky Native Plant Society.

Populus trichocarpa J.S. Peterson @ USDA-NRCS PLANTS Database.

Pseudotsuga menziesii J.S. Peterson @ USDA-NRCS PLANTS Database (both).

Cover photo: Zeland Studio, 615 Fort Street, Boise, Idaho. Ann DeBolt.

Index by Growth Form

	Scientific Name	Common Name	Family	Page Number
52	*Leymus cinereus*	Great Basin Wildrye	Poaceae	15
53	*Pseudoroegneria spicata*	Bluebunch Wheatgrass	Poaceae	15
54	*Sporobolus cryptandrus*	Sand Dropseed	Poaceae	15

SHRUBS

	Scientific Name	Common Name	Family	Page Number
55	*Acer glabrum*	Rocky Mountain Maple	Aceraceae	16
56	*Amelanchier alnifolia*	Saskatoon Serviceberry	Rosaceae	16
57	*Arctostaphylos uva-ursi*	Kinnikinnick	Ericaceae	16
58	*Artemisia cana*	Silver Sagebrush	Asteraceae	16
59	*Artemisia frigida*	Fringed Sagebrush	Asteraceae	17
60	*Artemisia ludoviciana*	Louisiana Sage	Asteraceae	17
61	*Artemisia tridentata*	Big Sagebrush	Asteraceae	17
62	*Atriplex canescens*	Four-wing Saltbush	Chenopodiaceae	17
63	*Cercocarpus ledifolius*	Curl-leaf Mountain Mahogany	Rosaceae	18
64	*Cercocarpus montanus*	Birch-leaf Mountain Mahogany	Rosaceae	18
65	*Chamaebatiaria millefolium*	Fern Bush	Rosaceae	18
66	*Chrysothamnus nauseosus*	Rubber Rabbitbrush	Asteraceae	18
67	*Chrysothamnus viscidiflorus*	Green Rabbitbrush	Asteraceae	19
68	*Cornus stolonifera*	Red-osier Dogwood	Cornaceae	19
69	*Crataegus douglasii*	Douglas Hawthorn	Rosaceae	19
70	*Ephedra viridis*	Mormon Tea	Ephedraceae	19
71	*Fallugia paradoxa*	Apache Plume	Rosaceae	19
72	*Krascheninnikovia lanata*	Winterfat	Chenopodiaceae	20
73	*Mahonia repens*	Creeping Oregon Grape	Berberidaceae	20
74	*Philadelphus lewisii*	Mockorange, Syringa	Hydrangeaceae	20
75	*Physocarpus malvaceus*	Ninebark	Rosaceae	20
76	*Potentilla fruticosa*	Shrubby Cinquefoil	Rosaceae	20
77	*Prunus emarginata*	Bitter Cherry	Rosaceae	21
78	*Prunus virginiana*	Chokecherry	Rosaceae	21
79	*Purshia tridentata*	Antelope Bitterbrush	Rosaceae	21
80	*Rhus glabra*	Smooth Sumac	Anacardiaceae	21
81	*Rhus trilobata*	Oakleaf Sumac	Anacardiaceae	22
82	*Ribes aureum*	Golden Currant	Grossulariaceae	22
83	*Ribes sanguineum*	Red-flowering Currant	Grossulariaceae	22
84	*Rosa woodsii*	Woods' Rose	Rosaceae	22
85	*Sambucus caerulea*	Blue Elderberry	Caprifoliaceae	23
86	*Shepherdia argentea*	Silver Buffaloberry	Elaeagnaceae	23
87	*Shepherdia canadensis*	Russet Buffaloberry	Elaeagnaceae	23
88	*Symphoricarpos albus*	Common Snowberry	Caprifoliaceae	23

TREES

	Scientific Name	Common Name	Family	Page Number
89	*Acer grandidentatum*	Big-tooth Maple	Aceraceae	24
90	*Betula occidentalis*	Water Birch	Betulaceae	24
91	*Celtis reticulata*	Netleaf Hackberry	Ulmaceae	24
92	*Juniperus occidentalis*	Western Juniper	Cupressaceae	24
93	*Larix occidentalis*	Western Larch	Pinaceae	24
94	*Picea pungens*	Blue Spruce	Pinaceae	24
95	*Pinus edulis*	Pinyon Pine	Pinaceae	25
96	*Pinus monticola*	Western White Pine	Pinaceae	25
97	*Pinus ponderosa*	Ponderosa Pine	Pinaceae	25
98	*Populus tremuloides*	Quaking Aspen	Salicaceae	25
99	*Populus trichocarpa*	Black Cottonwood	Salicaceae	26
100	*Pseudotsuga menziesii*	Douglas Fir	Pinaceae	26
101	*Sorbus scopulina*	Rocky Mountain Ash	Rosaceae	26

Index by Scientific Name

Index by Common Name

Common Name	Scientific Name	Family	Page Number
Pine-leaf Penstemon	*Penstemon pinifolius*	Scrophulariaceae	9
Pinyon Pine	*Pinus edulis*	Pinaceae	25
Ponderosa Pine	*Pinus ponderosa*	Pinaceae	25
Prairie Clover	*Petalostemon purpureum*	Fabaceae	10
Prairie Smoke	*Geum triflorum*	Rosaceae	6
Prickly Pear Cactus	*Opuntia* spp.	Cactaceae	8
Prince's Plume	*Stanleya pinnata*	Brassicaceae	11
Purple Coneflower	*Echinacea purpurea*	Asteraceae	5
Pussytoes	*Antennaria* spp.	Asteraceae	3
Quaking Aspen	*Populus tremuloides*	Salicaceae	25
Red-flowering Currant	*Ribes sanguineum*	Grossulariaceae	22
Red-osier Dogwood	*Cornus stolonifera*	Cornaceae	19
Rocky Mountain Ash	*Sorbus scopulina*	Rosaceae	26
Rocky Mountain Maple	*Acer glabrum*	Aceraceae	16
Rocky Mountain Penstemon	*Penstemon strictus*	Scrophulariaceae	10
Rubber Rabbitbrush	*Chrysothamnus nauseosus*	Asteraceae	18
Russet Buffaloberry	*Shepherdia canadensis*	Elaeagnaceae	23
Rydberg's Penstemon	*Penstemon rydbergii*	Scrophulariaceae	9
Sand Dropseed	*Sporobolus cryptandrus*	Poaceae	15
Saskatoon Serviceberry	*Amelanchier alnifolia*	Rosaceae	16
Scarlet Bugler	*Penstemon barbatus*	Scrophulariaceae	8
Scarlet Gilia	*Ipomopsis aggregata*	Polemoniaceae	7
Sheep Fescue	*Festuca ovina*	Poaceae	14
Showy Penstemon	*Penstemon speciosus*	Scrophulariaceae	10
Shrubby Cinquefoil	*Potentilla fruticosa*	Rosaceae	20
Shrubby Penstemon	*Penstemon fruticosus*	Scrophulariaceae	9
Silver Buffaloberry	*Shepherdia argentea*	Elaeagnaceae	23
Silver Lupine	*Lupinus argenteus*	Fabaceae	7
Silver Sagebrush	*Artemisia cana*	Asteraceae	16
Smooth Sumac	*Rhus glabra*	Anacardiaceae	21
Snow Buckwheat	*Eriogonum niveum*	Polygonaceae	5
Sticky Geranium	*Geranium viscosissimum*	Geraniaceae	6
Sulfur Buckwheat	*Eriogonum umbellatum*	Polygonaceae	6
Texas Red Yucca	*Hesperaloe parviflora*	Agavaceae	6
Water Birch	*Betula occidentalis*	Betulaceae	24
Western Columbine	*Aquilegia formosa*	Ranunculaceae	4
Western Juniper	*Juniperus occidentalis*	Cupressaceae	24
Western Larch	*Larix occidentalis*	Pinaceae	24
Western White Pine	*Pinus monticola*	Pinaceae	25
Western Yarrow	*Achillea millefolium*	Asteraceae	3
Whipple's Penstemon	*Penstemon whippleanus*	Scrophulariaceae	10
Wild Aster	*Aster* spp.	Asteraceae	4
Wild Blue Flax	*Linum perenne*	Linaceae	7
Winterfat	*Krascheninnikovia lanata*	Chenopodiaceae	20
Woods' Rose	*Rosa woodsii*	Rosaceae	22
Woolly Sunflower	*Eriophyllum lanatum*	Asteraceae	6
Wyeth Buckwheat	*Eriogonum heracleoides*	Polygonaceae	5

REPORT DOCUMENTATION PAGE

Form Approved
OMB No. 0704-0188

| 1. AGENCY USE ONLY (Leave blank) | 2. REPORT DATE
November 2003 | 3. REPORT TYPE AND DATES COVERED
Final |
|---|---|---|

4. TITLE AND SUBTITLE
TR-1730-3   Landscaping with Native Plants of the Intermountain Region

5. FUNDING NUMBERS

6. AUTHOR(S)
Hilary Parkinson

7. PERFORMING ORGANIZATION NAME(S) AND ADDRESS(ES)
U.S. Department of the Interior
Bureau of Land Management
National Science and Technology Center
P.O. Box 25047
Denver, CO 80225-0047

8. PERFORMING ORGANIZATION REPORT NUMBER
BLM/ID/ST-01/001+1730-3

9. SPONSORING / MONITORING AGENCY NAME(S) AND ADDRESS(ES)
Boise State University
Idaho Native Plant Society

10. SPONSORING / MONITORING AGENCY REPORT NUMBER

11. SUPPLEMENTARY NOTES

12a. DISTRIBUTION / AVAILABILITY STATEMENT

12b. DISTRIBUTION CODE

13. ABSTRACT *(Maximum 200 words)*
To promote the use of native plants in landscaping, this guide describes the characteristics and cultural requirements of 101 wildflower, grass, shrub, and tree species that were chosen based on their relative ease of growth, availability, and ornamental value. Each species featured includes information on the recommended amount of sun, water, whether deciduous or evergreen, cold hardiness, height and width, color and time of bloom, unusual characteristics or cultural preferences (such as preferred soil conditions), value to wildlife when applicable, with ancillary notes on any significant cultural, medicinal, or homeopathic uses. Many of the recommended plants are native to the Boise area, but all are native to the Intermountain Region, the Southwest, or the Great Plains. Information on xeriscaping, landscaping to reduce the risk of fire, plant recommendations for specific sites (plants for full sun, dry shade, etc.) and sources for native plants is also included. The material is designed for the homeowner, landscape contractor, business owner, school, etc., that seek to incorporate native plants in their landscape for their numerous values such as drought tolerance, value to wildlife, invasive weed reduction, historical and cultural significance and inherent beauty.
Total: 188 words (200 max)

14. SUBJECT TERMS
Native plants, gardening, landscaping, xeriscaping, firewise, drought tolerant, landscaping for wildlife, birds, hummingbirds, butterflies, lawn reduction, water conservation, Intermountain Region, west, southwest.

15. NUMBER OF PAGES
52 pages and covers

16. PRICE CODE

17. SECURITY CLASSIFICATION OF REPORT	18. SECURITY CLASSIFICATION OF THIS PAGE	19. SECURITY CLASSIFICATION OF ABSTRACT	20. LIMITATION OF ABSTRACT
Unclassified	Unclassified	Unclassified	UL